THE FIRST AMENDMENT
ON CAMPUS

NASPA

Student Affairs Administrators
in Higher Education

EDITED BY

LEE E. BIRD, MARY BETH MACKIN

& SAUNDRA K. SCHUSTER

THE FIRST AMENDMENT
ON CAMPUS

A Handbook

For College and University

Administrators

NASPA
Student Affairs Administrators
in Higher Education

The material presented in this book is intended to provide background information and decision models for addressing First Amendment issues. The material is not intended to provide legal advice. Institutional legal counsel should be consulted to provide the appropriate legal advice based upon each unique set of facts presented.

The First Amendment on Campus:
A Handbook for College and University Administrators
Copyright © 2006 by the National Association of Student Personnel Administrators (NASPA), Inc. Printed and bound in the United States of America. All rights reserved. No part of this book may be reproduced in any form or by any electronic or mechanical means without written permission from the publisher. First edition.

NASPA does not discriminate on the basis of race, color, national origin, religion, sex, age, affectional or sexual orientation, or disability in any of its policies, programs, and services.

Additional copies may be purchased by contacting the NASPA publications department at 301-638-1749 or visiting http://www.naspa. org/publications.

ISBN 0-931654-46-7

This book is dedicated to
the memory of

James M. Bird

Peace and Justice advocate.

TABLE OF CONTENTS

Impact on the Community
Creating a Plan of Action
Dealing with the Media
Practical Application

HEALING COMMUNITIES AND STAKEHOLDERS

Lee E. Bird and Mary Beth Mackin

At the Onset of the Incident
In the Weeks that Follow
The Aftermath
Bibliography

IMPORTANT CASES RELATED TO FREE SPEECH ON CAMPUS

Greg C. Lukianoff

RECOMMENDED RESOURCES FOR FIRST AMENDMENT ISSUES

Elizabeth M. Baldizan

ASJA FIRST AMENDMENT SURVEY

Elizabeth M. Baldizan and Roger R. Lee

Acknowledgements

We would like to thank the following individuals and groups for their contributions to this book: Jill Rucker and Kathy Shelton, Office of the Vice President for Student Affairs at Oklahoma State University, who kept us on track with manuscripts and schedules; Dr. Donald Gehring, who suggested that ASJA form a First Amendment Committee to survey members' understanding of First Amendment issues; and The Advanced Track of the Donald D. Gehring Campus Judicial Affairs Training Institute who helped us test and evaluate material used in the handbook.

CHAPTER ONE

First Amendment Challenges Across Time

*"We are not afraid to entrust the American
people with unpleasant facts, foreign ideas,
alien philosophies, and competitive values.
For a nation that is afraid to let its people
judge the truth and falsehood in an open
market is a nation that is afraid
of its people."*

President John F. Kennedy

The First Amendment

*Congress shall make no law respecting an
establishment of religion, or prohibiting the
free exercise thereof; or abridging the freedom
of speech, or of the press; or the right of the
people peaceably to assemble, and to petition
the Government for a redress of grievances.*

**The Constitution
of the United States of America**

THE PURPOSE OF THIS BOOK

This book presents advice and guidance based on previous court
cases and the experience of administrators and campus hearing
officers who have dealt with difficult First Amendment issues and
lived to tell about it. Every situation is different, and campus policies,
politics, and climate may also differ, necessitating careful analysis and
thoughtful action specific to an individual campus and the particular
First Amendment challenge. This book's scenarios, definitions, and
review of court cases can be used to help campus administrators work
through possible scenarios before they occur or may serve as useful
references in the throes of an issue. This guide goes beyond describ-
ing what an institution cannot or should not do in the face of a First
Amendment challenge (and there are many such challenges) to discuss-

ing strategies for dealing with myriad challenges and opportunities inherent in campus First Amendment debates and issues.

Everyone's attitudes, beliefs, and values are different. Our ability to maintain, have challenged, or even change what we believe, and the opportunity to share those beliefs freely with others is a right established by our Constitution. It is a right that colleges and universities should aggressively protect and preserve for generations of students to come. Conservative, liberal, Christian, pagan, gay, straight, or other, students come to campus to broaden their horizons, be exposed to new ideas and images, and create or continue to build a set of values and beliefs that will sustain them for a lifetime.

The authors of the Bill of Rights could never have imagined all of the cultural, social, economic, and political shifts and crises our country (and college campuses, for that matter) would experience in the centuries that would follow. Fortunately, they did know, however, that the language in the First Amendment provided our country with its best hope of growing and changing, as well as preventing the United States from becoming a totalitarian society.

Today, most college and university administrators recognize and support the benefits of having a diverse student body, but this was not always the case. For some colleges, integration (allowing African Americans to attend predominantly White institutions) didn't begin until the 1950s. The civil rights protests in the 1960s that disrupted campuses and cities across the nation helped change the legal discrimination that was the status quo and created monumental social change. Both sides of the debate were loud and sometimes destructive, but throughout the debate, true, lasting, and positive change occurred. While current campus free expression issues may not appear to have the same social significance, the free exchange of ideas remains the most powerful mechanism for change. Such free expression, however, is not always universally celebrated.

Although faculty, students, and administrators may not always agree on the value of controversial ideas, it is clear that restriction of such expression may have an even greater price. Nat Hentoff, quoting Bruno Schmidt, president of Yale University, wrote:

> "The first victims of such suppression are the students and faculty who do not have their own convictions tempered by exposure to other points of view, even if ultimately unpersuasive, but the more serious loss is suffered by the university because these acts of suppression tend to contribute to a pall of conformity on many campuses. And yet, most universities...do not...respond as if their academic integrity is threatened by these disruptions. Even in an open society, history demonstrates that freedom of speech needs firm protection to flourish. Free speech and unorthodox thinking are for most people easily intimidated, and especially so in the close confines of the university.

> "To stifle expression because it is obnoxious, erroneous, embarrassing, not instrumental to some political or ideological end is—quite apart from the invasion of the rights of others—a disastrous reflection on the idea of the university. It is to elevate fear over the capacity for a liberated humane mind." (Hentoff, 1992, p. 134-135)

CIVILITY AT RISK?

Campus incidents involving First Amendment issues often seem to pit the protection of individual rights, guaranteed under the Constitution, against the need for preserving basic civility and maintaining productive living and learning environments. While some authors have talked about finding the "right balance" between the two, the reality is that when there is a perceived conflict, educators and administrators at public institutions of higher education should be the first to recognize and protect the First Amendment, even when such actions can invite additional campus conflict as well as litigation. Developing an understanding of the elements of the First Amendment and related court decisions will serve campus administrators well during such times.

Over the last several years, numerous authors and watchdog groups have condemned college and university administrators for their ignorance regarding First Amendment rights. In her book, *The New Thought Police,* Tammy Bruce wrote:

> Ironically, colleges and universities, once the champions of freedom of expression and the leaders in encouraging genuine dialogue and inquiry, are now implementing the opposite. The liberal university culture has turned into, as one valiant professor put it 'the slithering gargoyle it once fought against—the oppressive Establishment. (Bruce, 2001, p. 210-211)

The Foundation for Individual Rights in Education (FIRE) has also taken higher education, more specifically, public institutions, to task for violating the First Amendment rights of students, often attributing some degree of malicious intent.

> Unfortunately, ironically, and sadly, America's colleges and universities are all too often dedicated more to indoctrination and censorship than to freedom and indi-

5

vidual self government. As colleges are frequently places where majority rule means that minorities are silenced, and where notions of "diversity" and "tolerance"— which should expand the domains of liberty and difference—are twisted into justifications for suppressing any speech that differs from or offends the university's official orthodoxy in matters of politics or world view. In order to protect "diversity" and to ensure "tolerance," university officials proclaim, views deemed hostile or offensive to *some* students and *some* persuasions (and, indeed, some administrators) are subjected to censorship under campus codes. (French, Lukianoff & Silverglate, 2005, p. 2-3)

College and university administrators may truly be confused about the right course of action when encountering First Amendment issues on campus. While some issues may be viewed as more "black and white," others fall into grey areas and are judged and acted upon in the larger context of time, campus demographics, culture, regional and national politics, and other factors that drive campus decision making. *FIRE's Guide to Free Speech on Campus* (French, et al., 2005) offers an excellent history of key First Amendment challenges that illustrates how various groups have ignored the First Amendment to protect their positions rather than engage in free and open debate. For example, "Southern politicians argued that the antislavery speech tended to produce slave revolts, that it threatened the cohesiveness of the Union. And, even, that the speech of abolitionists 'inflicted emotional injury' on the slave owners" (French, et al., p. 10).

As Justice Hugo Black said, "The layman's constitutional view is that what he likes is constitutional and that which he doesn't like is unconstitutional"(*New York Times*, Feb. 26, 1971).

Higher education law is complex and open to varying interpretations. In addition, campuses are dynamic institutions affected by the politics and policies of the day, which can result in a clash of values, interests, and the law. Determining the most appropriate course of action in the midst of these competing interests and the law is difficult at best, and decision makers may find themselves in a campus crisis without clear direction and with growing pressure to take action. Three examples will help illustrate this point. The first comes from *Doe v. University of Michigan* (1989). In response to increased diversity on campus, the university received a growing number of complaints that students of color were being verbally abused on campus and that the university had an obligation to do something about it. Feeling as though they had the backing of legislation preventing racial discrimination in education (Title VI), administrators penned one of the earliest known "speech codes" or "hate speech codes," as they were called. The codes were written to try to prevent speech and actions that were thought to create a hostile environment that made it difficult, if not impossible, for some students to benefit from the programs and services offered by the university and obtain an education, thereby discriminating against them. Such codes were written in good faith to try to reduce a perceived threat to the university's strong desire to increase the diversity of the student body and faculty and staff ranks, prevent the aforementioned discrimination, and maintain a more positive living and learning environment. When tested, the U.S. district court ruled that the policy was "overbroad" as written and applied and created a "chilling effect," which might limit legitimate, yet controversial, speech, and the Court prohibited the university from continuing its use. (See also *Dambrot* and *The UWM Post, Inc.* in Chapter Eight.)

The second example involves not so subtle changes in how the

High Court hears a case or, in this example, refuses to hear a case. Most readers have heard of the *Papish v. Board of Curators of the University of Missouri* case involving the student editor of the school newspaper whose choice of satirical political cartoons deeply angered the administration and the public. The cartoon, which depicted a police officer raping the Statue of Liberty and the Goddess of Justice, related to a story in the paper with the headline "Mother Fucker Acquitted." In response to the outcry and demands that the administration take action, the editor was promptly expelled, having been charged with violating a murky code prohibiting "indecent conduct or speech." The Supreme Court overturned the suspension of the student stating that "the mere dissemination of ideas—no matter how offensive to good taste—on a state university campus may not be shut off in the name alone of 'conventions of decency.'" In this ruling, the Court made a distinction between any form of censorship of high school newspapers and those of a college or university. While the Court did not like what was printed, which is clear from their opinions, it determined that protecting the First Amendment served a greater interest than protecting those offended by the cartoon or the article headline.

Now move to a recent case, *Hosty v. Carter,* involving Governors State University in Illinois. David Epstein, reporting for an article in *Inside Higher Ed*, indicated that Dean of Student Services Patricia Carter blocked the printing of articles that were critical of the administration unless she reviewed them first. The paper sued and felt quite confident in doing so based on earlier and consistent court decisions that were supportive of the right of colleges and universities to write the news and commentary without such scrutiny. However, the Seventh Circuit, sitting *en banc*, gave great deference to the school officials to determine what was educationally appropriate material for the campus newspaper. The Court applied an analysis similar to the K–12 case *Hazelwood School District v. Kuhlmeier*, in which the Supreme Court determined that the school could supervise and determine the content of its student newspaper, based on the concept that when a school regulates speech for which it also pays, the appropriate question is whether the actions are reasonably related to legitimate pedagogical concerns. However, in this case the Court also stated in a footnote that they would not decide the same degree of deference was appropriate for similar activities at the college or university level. Most lower courts since 1988 have declined to apply this limitation in the higher education arena. The reporters appealed to the Supreme Court, which declined to hear the appeal.

Epstein interviewed Mark Goodman, executive director of the Student Press Law Center, for the article:

> To suggest that an adult on a college campus can be treated the same way as a 14-year-old can in high school...signals the potential beginning of major erosion of college and university First Amendment rights. Goodman added that the Supreme Court has been protective of free expression on campus for the last 30 years, beginning with *Healy v. James* in 1972, when the Court defended the college environment as 'peculiarly the marketplace of ideas' in need of uninhibited expression. (Epstein, 2006)

Is freedom of the press truly in jeopardy? Will this ruling (applicable only in the states within its jurisdiction) serve as precedent in cases to come? Without a doubt, such apparently random decisions make one wonder if the courts, in this case, have a uniform understanding of college newspaper funding and public forums.

Another area of confusion has surged into the forefront involving sexual harassment (gender discrimination under Title IX). What exactly is protected speech and what is sexual harassment? This issue has come nearly full circle in the last few years and provides the third example. Following sexual harassment cases such as *Gebser* and *Davis*, the Department of Education's Office for Civil Rights (OCR) provided guidance to help colleges and universities prevent sexual harassment (defined as a continuum of behaviors ranging from verbal harassment based on gender to sexual violence). Published in 2001, *Revised Sexual Harassment Guidance: Harassment of Students By School Employees, Other Students, or Third Parties* established that colleges and universities need to:

1. Establish a specific policy regarding sexual harassment

2. Inform the campus community of said policy

3. Take action to stop the harassment, prevent its recurrence and make the person affected whole to the extent possible so that the effects of the discrimination can be ameliorated. (OCR, 2001, p. 23)

The guidance covered penalties for ignoring sexual harassment on or off campus involving faculty-to-student harassment, student-to-student harassment, and even total strangers (visitors) on campus.

The new guidance also established that administrators and other key officials could be liable for monetary damages if they knew about sexual harassment (or should have known) and were deliberately indifferent to the plight of the victim(s). In addition to providing this clarification, the document also illustrated numerous examples of speech and behavior that, on their face and taken alone, did not rise to the level of sexual harassment, which is defined as unwelcome conduct based on gender that is severe and pervasive and limits a student's ability to benefit from the programs and services provided by the university. Just as before, colleges and universities wrote codes and offered sexual harassment training. Colleges tried to define and describe conduct based on this guidance, which left administrators confused about what they could or could not say or do.

College campuses were not alone in their confusion. FIRE effectively challenged the OCR on its guidance, noting that many of the examples reflected protected speech. In response, the OCR wrote a letter that attempted to clarify the confusion between protected and harassing speech. In essence, it makes clear that, when in doubt, the First Amendment trumps Title IX and that OCR regulations regarding sexual harassment are not intended to "restrict the exercise of any expressive activities protected under the U.S. Constitution." The text of that letter, which was signed by the OCR's assistant secretary, follows.

> I am writing to confirm the position of the Office for Civil Rights (OCR) of the U.S. Department of Education regarding a subject which is of central importance to our government, our heritage of freedom, and our way of life: the First Amendment of the U.S. Constitution.
>
> OCR has received inquiries regarding whether OCR's regulations are intended to restrict speech activities that are protected under the First Amendment. I want to assure you in the clearest possible terms that OCR's regulations are not intended to restrict the exercise of any expressive activities protected under the U.S. Constitution. OCR has consistently maintained that the statutes that it enforces are intended to protect students from invidious discrimination, not to regulate the content

of speech. Harassment of students, which can include verbal or physical conduct, can be a form of discrimination prohibited by the statutes enforced by OCR. Thus, for example, in addressing harassment allegations, OCR has recognized that the offensiveness of a particular expression, standing alone, is not a legally sufficient basis to establish a hostile environment under the statutes enforced by OCR. In order to establish a hostile environment, harassment must be sufficiently serious (i.e., severe, persistent or pervasive) as to limit or deny a student's ability to participate in or benefit from an educational program. OCR has consistently maintained that schools in regulating the conduct of students and faculty to prevent or redress discrimination must formulate, interpret, and apply their rules in a manner that respects the legal rights of students and faculty, including those court precedents interpreting the concept of free speech. OCR's regulations and policies do not require or prescribe speech, conduct or harassment codes that impair the exercise of rights protected under the First Amendment.

As you know, OCR enforces several statutes that prohibit discrimination on the basis of sex, race or other prohibited classifications in federally funded educational programs and activities. These prohibitions include racial, disability and sexual harassment of students. Let me emphasize that OCR is committed to the full, fair and effective enforcement of these statutes consistent with the requirements of the First Amendment. Only by eliminating these forms of discrimination can we fully ensure that every student receives an equal opportunity to achieve academic excellence.

Some colleges and universities have interpreted OCR's prohibition of "harassment" as encompassing all offensive speech regarding sex, disability, race or other classifications. Harassment, however, to be prohibited by the statutes within OCR's jurisdiction, must include something beyond the mere expression of views, words, symbols or thoughts that some person finds offensive. Under OCR's standard, the conduct must also be considered sufficiently serious to deny or limit a student's ability to participate in or benefit from the educational program. Thus, OCR's standards require that the conduct be evaluated from the perspective of a reasonable person in the alleged victim's position, considering all the circumstances, including the alleged victim's age.

There has been some confusion arising from the fact that OCR's regulations are enforced against private institutions that receive federal funds. Because the First Amendment normally does not bind private institutions, some have erroneously assumed that OCR's regulations apply to private federal-funds recipients without the constitutional limitations imposed on public institutions. OCR's regulations should not be interpreted in ways that would lead to the suppression of protected speech on public or private campuses. Any private postsecondary institution that chooses to limit free speech in ways that are more restrictive than at public educational institutions does so on its own accord and not based on requirements imposed by OCR.

In summary, OCR interprets its regulations consistent with the requirements of the First Amendment, and all actions taken by OCR must comport with First Amendment principles. No OCR regulation should be interpreted to impinge upon rights protected under the First Amendment to the U.S. Constitution or to require recipients to enact or enforce codes that punish the exercise of such rights. There is no conflict between the civil rights laws that this Office enforces and the civil liberties guaranteed by the First Amendment. With these principles in mind, we can, consistent with the requirements of the First Amendment, ensure a safe and nondiscriminatory environment for students that is conducive to learning and protects both the constitutional and civil rights of all students. (OCR, 2003)

OUR DESIRE TO DO THE "RIGHT" THING...AND WHAT WOULD THAT BE?

"Free speech for me but not for thee," provides a great metaphor for First Amendment issues on campus. Do administrators block, discourage, or attempt to adjudicate speech because it doesn't agree with their belief systems or institutional mission statements? What do administrators do when the First Amendment seemingly conflicts with tightly held institutional values? Administrators might believe that supporting diversity and civility on campus is more important than protecting the speech of someone on the mall spouting his/her version of hate toward some underrepresented group. After all, a given campus may have worked very hard to market the institution as welcoming, diverse, and inclusive, and incidents that cause people to feel unwelcome or "targeted" will likely create student unrest and invite criticism from internal and external constituents alike. Many administrators have struggled with these and similar dilemmas. They weigh the options and possible outcomes, one against the other, and hope beyond hope that they will make the right decisions.

Administrators may struggle with campus policies created to comply with federal law prohibiting sexual and racial harassment, only to find that they face a First Amendment challenge from one of several watchdog groups. When policies or laws seem to conflict, which takes precedence? Campuses have used a large share of resources teaching staff, administrators, faculty, and students how to prevent and/or respond to sexual and racial harassment leading to discrimination. However, few campuses spend any resources talking about protecting the First Amendment and responding to and managing challenges. FIRE has taken the position that campuses disregard the First Amendment to avoid controversy. Although this may not be true, based on the experience of some of this book's authors, upholding the First Amendment may indeed serve (at least initially) as a lightning rod for chaos.

THE BALANCING TEST

When faced with incivility on campus, what administrators feel is the right thing to do as educators and kind human beings may conflict with the legally appropriate thing to do. At this juncture, a metaphor might be helpful. The best description for evaluating First Amendment issues, especially for public institutions, comes from examining the *balancing test* that will be described more fully in Chapter Two. In essence, the test is used to weigh whether the government's interest in content-neutral regulation of speech and related conduct outweighs the speaker's or listener's interest in a particular form of communication. The balancing test begins with the court placing a thumb on the side of free expression (Emanual, 2003). When administrators begin to examine expression—verbal or symbolic—on their campuses, this metaphor should remind them that the First Amendment protects all voices, even those that someone may find irresponsible, defiant, or oppressive. For every person who finds a voice irresponsible, defiant, or oppressive, another will find it a rousing example of free speech.

The following quotes clearly articulate the position of various courts and scholars with regard to the power and promise of the First Amendment and have been selected to help readers understand that the court's "thumb" is purposefully imposing!

> The Supreme Court has said that the nature and principal function under our system of government is to invite disputes, and that it may indeed best serve its high purpose when it induces a condition of unrest, creates dissatisfaction with conditions as they are or even stirs people to anger. The freedoms of speech and of press are fundamental personal rights and liberties, the exercise of which lies at the foundation of a free government by free people. It is only through free debate and free exchange of ideas that the government remains responsive to the will of the people and peaceful change is effected. The right to speak freely and to promote a diversity of ideas and programs is therefore one of the chief distinctions that sets the United States apart from totalitarian regimes. (Justice William Douglas, *Terminiello v. City of Chicago*)

...the First Amendment does not permit the government to restrict the speech of some elements of society in order to enhance the relative voice of others. Freedom of speech and of the press rests on the assumption that the widest possible dissemination of information from diverse and antagonistic sources is essential to the welfare of the public. (*American Jurisprudence*, 2005)

As far back as 1929, Justice Holmes, dissenting in *United States v. Schwimmer*, penned one of the most often-quoted phrases in American constitutional law when he called for the principle of free thought—not free thought for those who agree with us, but freedom for the thought we hate. Harvard Law School constitution scholar Laurence Tribe wrote in the 1988 edition of his acclaimed constitutional law treatise that if the Constitution forces government to allow people to march, speak and write in favor of peace, brotherhood, and justice, then it must also require government to allow them to advocate hatred, racism and even genocide. (Kors and Silverglate, 1999, p. 47)

Writing in the *Cohen* decision, Justice John M. Harlan said:

The Constitutional right of free expression is powerful medicine in a society as diverse and populous as ours. It is designed and intended to remove governmental restraints from the arena of public discussion, putting the decision as to what views shall be voiced largely in the hands of each other, in the hopes that use of such freedom will ultimately produce a capable citizenry and more perfect polity and in the belief that no other approach would comport with the premise of individual dignity and choice upon which our political system rests. (Irons, 1997, p. 83)

Justice Hugo Black wrote:

The greater the importance of safeguarding the community from incitements to the overthrow of our institutions by force and violence, the more imperative is the need to preserve inviolate the constitutional rights of free speech, free press and free assembly in order to maintain the opportunity for free political discussion, to the end that government may be responsive to the will of the people and that changes, if desired, may be obtained by peaceful means. Therein lies the security of the Republic, the very foundation of constitutional government. (Irons, p. 196)

Harlan emphasized the value of freedom of speech in developing a more capable citizenry and recognizing the premise of individual dignity on which our system rests. These values are served even when speech is tumultuous and offensive; "that the air may at times seem filled with verbal cacophony is, in this sense not a sign of weakness but of strength." (Barron and Dienes, 2004, p. 91)

Freedom of expression is essential to democratic government. Without free speech, citizens cannot debate the actions and policies of their elected officials, nor can they be well informed about current issues. Thus, some people argue that the First Amendment protects only political speech. But others maintain that freedom of speech is not limited to politics, but includes art, music, literature, science, and business. (Monk, 1991, p. 59)

Americans are a diverse and often disputatious people. They belong to many religions and to none; they speak their minds on every issue that invites argument; they publish thousands of newspapers, magazines, and leaflets; and they march and picket for a multitude of causes that span the political spectrum. Every American city or town has its zealots and dissenters, who often press their views on other citizens in ways that some find annoying or disruptive. Many people resent doorbell ringers, street-corner orators, gossip tabloids, and placard wavers. But we generally tolerate those who set up shop in the "marketplace of ideas" that keeps us informed and fuels our debate on public issues.

But tolerance has its limits. Some ideas and opinions are so offensive to many people, that their expression is considered harmful to society. The limits of free expression raise tough questions. (Irons & Guitton, 1997, p. 57)

CHAPTER ONE

BIBLIOGRAPHY

American Jurisprudence 2d. State and Federal Constitutional Law. (2005). Stamford, CT: Lawyers Cooperative Publishing.

Barron, J. & Dienes, C.T. (2004). *First Amendment Law in a Nutshell* (3rd ed.). St. Paul, MN: West Publishing Company.

Bruce, T. (2005). *The New Thought Police.* Victoria, BC: Crown Publications.

Constitutional Convention Members. (1787). The Constitution of the United States of America [Electronic Version]. Retrieved July 6, 2006 from http://www.archives.gov/national-archives-experience/charters/constitution.html

Emanual, S. (2003). *Law Outlines: Constitutional Law.* New York City, NY: Aspen Publishers.

Epstein, D. (2006, Feb. 22). When Freedom Isn't Freedom at All. *Inside Higher Ed.* Retrieved July 7, 2006 from http://www.insidehighered.com/news/2006/02/22/supreme

French, D.A., Lukianoff, G. & Silverglate, H. A. (2005). *FIRE's Guide to Free Speech on Campus.* Philadelphia, PA: Foundation for Individual Rights in Education.

Hentoff, N. (1992). *Free Speech for Me But Not for Thee: How the American Left and Right Relentlessly Censor Each Other.* New York, NY: Harper Perennial.

Irons, P. (1997). *The First Amendment.* New York, NY: The New Press.

Irons, P. & Guitton, S. (1993). (Eds.). *May It Please the Court.* New York, NY The New Press.

20

Kors, A.C. & Silverglate, H.A. (1999). *The Shadow University: The Betrayal of Liberty on America's Campuses*. New York, NY: Harper Collins Publishers.

Monk, L.R. (1991). *The Bill of Rights: A User's Guide*. Alexandria, VA. Close Up Publishing.

Office for Civil Rights, Department of Education. (2001). *Revised Sexual Harassment Guidance: Harassment of Student by School Employees, Other Students or Third Parties* [Electronic Version]. Retrieved July 7, 2006 from http://www.ed.gov/legislation/FedRegister/other/2001-1/011901b.html

Office for Civil Rights, Department of Education. (2003, July 28). *First Amendment: Dear Colleague* [Electronic version]. Retrieved July 6, 2006 from http://www.ed.gov/about/offices/list/ocr/firstamend.html

CASES REFERENCED

Davis v. Monroe County Bd. of Educ., 526 U.S. 629 (1999)

Doe v. University of Michigan, 721F. SUPP. 852 (E.D.MICH. 1989)

Gebser v. Lago Vista Independent School District, 524 U.S. 274 (1998)

Hazelwood School District v. Kuhlmeier, 484 U.S. 260 (1988)

Healy v. James, 408 U.S. 169 (1972)

Hosty v. Carter, 412 F.3d 731 (2005)

Papish v. Board of Curators of the University of Missouri, 410 U.S. 667 (1973)

United States v. Schwimmer, 279 U.S. 644 (1929)

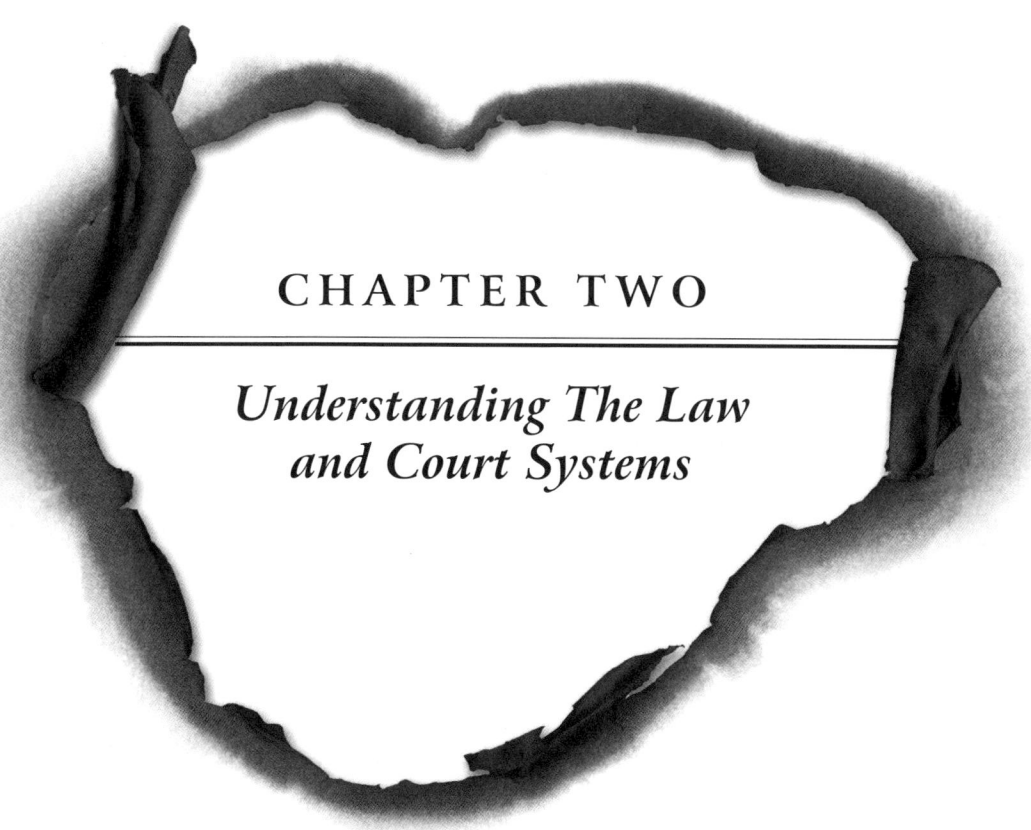

CHAPTER TWO

Understanding The Law and Court Systems

"When the [Supreme] Court moved to
Washington in 1800, it was provided with
no books, which probably accounts for the
high quality of early opinions."

Justice Robert H. Jackson

UNDERSTANDING THE COURT SYSTEMS

Although First Amendment issues are often difficult ones to deal with and may leave administrators struggling with how to respond, there are resources and precedents that may provide guidance. The most informative of these are undoubtedly the decisions and opinions of our nation's courts. Most free expression issues have occurred in some form previously and most have been analyzed and ruled upon, which provides precedent for the action that institutions might take. Developing a familiarity with such cases and an understanding of how to find them, as well as read and interpret their importance, will be beneficial to university administrators when determining how to proceed.

The numbers, letters, and cryptic abbreviations that follow a case citation may appear to be written in code. Actually, they provide a logical roadmap to the "who," "when," and "where" of the case at hand. Understanding the citation system is useful, not only for finding a case, but also for determining the significance and scope of the holding of the case. Why is an understanding of state and federal court decisions and the hierarchy within those courts important? Because the *holding*—or final decision—of a court will create *binding law* only on the specific physical area—or *jurisdiction*—in which the case was decided. Courts at all levels will take into consideration the holding and legal analysis of case decisions from other jurisdictions, but they are not "bound" or required to follow those decisions unless it was from their own jurisdiction. In fact, courts often use the phrase, "This decision is persuasive, but not binding." Therefore, understanding the level of the court that is making the decision and the jurisdiction will provide guidance about whether an institution is required to apply and follow the court's decision. A different jurisdiction's decision may be important because of what can be learned from it, but it does not require the institution to adhere to the ruling.

Cases are filed in both state and federal courts, based upon the law that has allegedly been violated. The state and federal courts generally function independently from each other, and both court systems have a hierarchy process that enables a party to the case to appeal the decision to the next highest court. Within both state and federal court systems, decisions of a "higher court" in the hierarchy will be binding on all lower courts in each jurisdiction. For example, an Ohio Supreme Court decision will be binding on all state courts in Ohio. In addition, a federal court decision will be binding on the specific jurisdiction of that court and will generally overrule any state court decisions that are contrary to that federal court decision (this concept is called the Supremacy Clause).

The decision of a state's highest court, usually but not always called a supreme court, can be appealed only to the U.S. Supreme Court. Appeals filed with the U.S. Supreme Court are always "discretionary," meaning that the Court decides if they are willing to hear an appeal or not. Generally, for the U.S. Supreme Court to agree to hear an appeal from a state's highest court, there must be a federal question involved, and four or more justices must agree to hear the case. Therefore, when you read that a *request for certiorari* (or *cert*) has been filed, it means that a request has been made to the U.S. Supreme Court to hear an appeal. The highest state courts also operate on a *cert* basis. That is, they decide if they want to hear a case or not. Though it rarely happens, a federal court may refer a case to a state court if the federal court feels that it would be more appropriate to apply state law to a case.

In state cases, a lawsuit is commenced in the *trial court* (also called

25

county court, common pleas court, or *superior court*). The specific jurisdiction for trial courts will vary from state to state; sometimes it's based on the county system in the state, and sometimes the state has set up a different way to carve up the state for court proceedings. An appeal from the trial court goes to the designated *court of appeals.* Not all states have courts of appeal, in which case, a decision of the trial court can be appealed directly to the state supreme court. In some states, these appeal courts are referred to as *district courts,* which have a broader base of jurisdiction than the trial court. The federal court system also has district courts, which is why it is important to know if a case is in a state or federal court. An appeal from a state court of appeals or state district court is appealed to the state's highest court. Generally, this is the end of the line for the decision, except in the rare case that a federal question of such significance arises, the U.S. Supreme Court agrees to hear the case.

In the federal court system, the United States is divided into *circuits.* Each circuit includes several states. Within the circuits are *district courts.* The district courts are the initial court in which to file a federal case (also known as the trial court). The hierarchy in the federal court system, like the state system, provides that a case decided at the district court level can be appealed to the *circuit court of appeals.* Circuit court decisions are appealed to the U.S. Supreme Court, which can choose whether or not to accept the case (take *cert*). A decision from the U.S. Supreme Court is binding across the United States and trumps any state or federal lower court decision that conflicts with the Supreme Court decision.

FEDERAL CIRCUITS

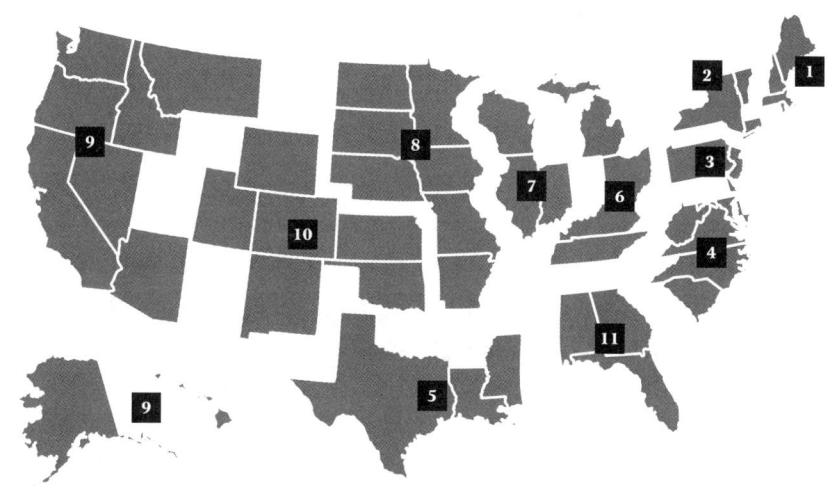

Source: Association for Student Judicial Affairs

UNDERSTANDING CASE LAW CITATIONS

Case law citations provide the legal reference to case decisions, which the following example illustrates.

Gay Student Services v. Texas A&M, 737 F.2d 1317 (5th Cir. 1984)

The first part of this citation (*Gay Student Services v. Texas A&M*) identifies the parties involved. When the case is at the trial court level, the party bringing the suit will be listed first. Next is the volume number (737), the case reporter name and the series number (F.2d), and the first page in the volume on which the case starts (1317). The case reporter is the document in which the case is published. "F." stands for *Federal Reporter*, which contains the 13 federal judicial circuit courts of appeal, and "2d" represents the volume of the *Federal Reporter*. Sometimes this part will state "F. Supp."

27

which means *Federal Supplement*, which signifies the case is from one of the federal district court decisions. The abbreviations "U.S." (*United States Reports*), "S.Ct." (*Supreme Court Reporter*), and "L.Ed." (*Lawyer's Edition*) all represent reporters that report U.S. Supreme Court decisions. In addition to the reporters discussed above for federal cases, there are a wide range of regional reporters for state cases, including "P." (*Pacific Reporter*), "A." (*Atlantic Reporter*), "N.E." (*Northeastern Reporter*), "N.W." (*Northwestern Reporter*), "S." (*Southern Reporter*), and "S.W." (*Southwestern Reporter*). Additionally, many states have their own state reporters. Some cases may have two or three reporter names so the case can be found in any of the reporters listed.

Some cases have a case citation that does not reference a reporter, but may reference another source for the location of the case report, for example: *Smith v. Career College*, No. 04-86-00267, LEXIS 45967 (Ohio App. 2003)

As with the federal cases, "*Smith v. Career College*" identifies the parties to the case; "No. 04-86-00267" refers to the court file number; "LEXIS 45967" is the number of the case (generally the first page) in the computerized database of LEXIS cases. WESTLAW is another database frequently referenced in cases and access to both of these databases may require a fee. Finally, "Ohio App. 2003" identifies the state court and the year the case was decided. Generally, one can look up a case on the Internet by using the case name, date of the decision, and the court file number or by asking a reference librarian for assistance.

COMMONLY USED LEGAL TERMS

Although there are often no clear-cut answers to First Amendment issues on campus, there are guidelines, concepts, and legal precedents to aid in determining the most appropriate (and defensible) courses of action. The terms below provide a useful context for the discussions and case scenarios that will be presented in subsequent chapters.

Academic freedom. The concept of academic freedom was created by the American Association of University Professors in its *1940 Statement of Principles on Academic Freedom and Tenure.* Academic freedom consists of a set of values that protect a faculty member's freedom of intellectual expression and inquiry. It was originally created as a means of advancing the search for truth, rather than as a manifestation of First Amendment rights. The term as used today encompasses much more than teaching-related speech rights of teachers (Black, 1991).

Balancing test. A constitutional doctrine in which the court weighs the rights of an individual as guaranteed by the Constitution with the rights of a state to protect its citizens from the invasion of their rights; used in cases involving freedom of speech and equal protection (Black, 1991). A court will apply a balancing test, using standards established by the U.S. Supreme Court, in cases involving a challenge alleging a violation of an individual's (group's) First Amendment rights. The test will apply either a strict scrutiny or rational basis test. (See definitions for "strict scrutiny" and "rational basis.")

Captive audience. Any group that is subject to a speaker or to a performance and is not free to depart without adverse consequences (Black, 1991).

Chilling effect. *Constitutional law.* 1. The result of a law or practice that seriously discourages the exercise of a constitutional right,

29

such as the right to appeal or the right of free speech. 2. Broadly, the result when any practice is discouraged (Black, 1999).

Chilling effect doctrine. In constitutional law, any law or practice that has the effect of seriously discouraging the exercise of a constitutional right. The deterrent effect of governmental action that falls short of a direct prohibition against the exercise of First Amendment rights. To constitute an impermissible chilling effect, the constrictive impact must arise from the present or future exercise or threatened exercise of coercive power (Black, 1991).

Compelling state interest test. *Constitutional law*. A method for determining the constitutional validity of a law, whereby the government's interest in the law is balanced against the individual's constitutional right to be free of the law. Only if the government's interest is strong enough will the law be upheld.

The U.S. Supreme Court has designated several rights of individuals that the governmental unit may only control or restrict through laws or policies if they serve a "compelling governmental (state) interest." The Court describes this form of balancing test as applying strict scrutiny (see definition for "strict scrutiny") to the law or policy (Black, 1999). If the governmental unit cannot provide this high level of scrutiny, then it will be determined to have violated the constitutionally protected right in question.

Content-based restriction. *Constitutional law*. A restraint on the substance of a particular type of speech. This type of restriction can survive a challenge only if it is based on a compelling state interest and its measures are narrowly drawn to accomplish that end (Black, 1999).

Defamation. An intentional false communication either published or publicly spoken, that injures another's reputation or good name. The holding up of a person to ridicule, scorn, or contempt in a respectable and considerable part of the community; may be criminal as well as civil. Includes both libel and slander.

a. Words that are false and untrue

b. Injury of character and reputation

c. Communication to third person

If the victim is a public official, reckless disregard must also be shown (Black, 1991).

Designated public forum. See "forum."

Establishment clause. The First Amendment provision that prohibits the government from creating or favoring a particular religion. U.S. Const. Amendment I (Black, 1991).

Fighting words. 1. Inflammatory speech that might not be protected by the First Amendment's free-speech guarantee because it might incite a violent response. 2. Inflammatory speech that is pleadable in mitigation—but not in defense—of a suit for assault (Black, 1999).

The seminal case regarding fighting words is *Chaplinsky v. New Hampshire*. Fighting words are those that, by their very utterance, inflict injury or tend to incite an immediate breach of the peace, having direct tendency to cause acts of violence by the persons to whom the remark is addressed. In *Chaplinsky* and a few cases since, the Court has applied a fighting words standard as an unprotected form of speech. This standard is seldom applied as our society has become generally more permissive and the standards of acceptable language have been eased. "The expression must be directed to inciting or producing imminent lawless action and be likely to incite or produce such action"

(*Brandenburg v. Ohio*). "No danger flowing from speech can be deemed clear and present, unless the incidence of the evil apprehended is so imminent that it may befall before there is opportunity for full discussion" (*Whitney v. California*).

First Amendment. The constitutional amendment, ratified with the Bill of Rights in 1791, guaranteeing the freedoms of speech, religion, press, assembly, and petition (Black, 1999).

Forum. n. 1. A public place, esp. one devoted to assembly or debate. 2. A court or other judicial body; a place of jurisdiction. Pl. forums, fora (Black, 1999).

Types of forums (from least controllable to most) include:

★ **Public forum**. *Constitutional law*. Public property where people traditionally gather to express ideas and exchange views. To be constitutional, the government's regulation of a public forum must be narrowly tailored to serve a significant government interest and must be limited to time, place, or manner restrictions (Black, 1991).

★ **Public forum**. n. A place that has long-standing tradition of being used for, is historically associated with, or has been dedicated by government act to the free exercise of the right to speech and public debate and assembly (*Legal Encyclopedia* [Electronic Version]).

The U.S. Supreme Court created a "forum analysis" in regard to the First Amendment as a means to determine when the government's interest in limiting the use of its property outweighs the interest of those wishing to use the property for other purposes. This includes:

★ **Traditional public forum.** Public property that has by long tradition—as opposed to governmental designation—been used by the public for assembly and expression, such as a public street, public sidewalk, or public park. To be constitutional, the government will apply the strict scrutiny standard of analysis, which requires that content-neutral restrictions of the time, place, or manner of expression meet the "compelling governmental interest standard." Any government regulation of expression that is based on the content of the expression must meet the highest constitutional test of being narrowly tailored to serve a compelling state interest (Black, 1999).

★ **Designated public forum.** Public property that has not traditionally been open for public assembly and debate, but that the government has opened for use by the public as a place for expressive activity, such as a public university facility or a publicly owned theater. A designated public forum is not created by inaction or simply permitting limited discourse. Instead, it must be created by **both policy and practice demonstrating intent.** Unlike a traditional public forum, the government does not have to retain the open character of a designated public forum (Black, 1999). Also, the subject matter of the expression permitted in a designated public forum may be limited to accord with the character of the forum; content-neutral time, place, and manner restrictions are generally permissible. But any prohibition based on the content of the expression must be narrowly drawn to effectuate a compelling state interest, as with a traditional public forum.

★ **Limited public forum.** A public forum created by the government voluntarily for expressive activity that may be restricted as to subject matter or class of speaker (*Legal Encyclopedia* [Electronic Version]).

★ The U.S. Supreme Court has designated this type of forum as a way for a governmental entity, such as a college or university, to create an environment for expression that is controlled by the mission of the institution. Thus, it can be designated as limited to particular groups or particular topics, as long as those restrictions are not based upon the content of the message to be delivered. The Court has identified the application of a rational basis or reasonableness standard of scrutiny to this type of forum as opposed to a strict scrutiny. The entity must still apply a content-neutral time, place, or manner standard.

Fourteenth Amendment. The constitutional amendment, ratified in 1868, whose primary provisions effectively apply the Bill of Rights to the states by forbidding states from denying due process and equal protection and from abridging the privileges and immunities of U.S. citizenship. The amendment also gives Congress the power to enforce these provisions, leading to legislation such as the Civil Rights Acts (Black, 1999).

Fourth Amendment. The constitutional amendment, ratified with the Bill of Rights in 1791, prohibiting unreasonable searches and seizures and the issuance of warrants without probable cause (Black, 1999).

Harassment. As defined in federal statute providing for a civil action to restrain harassment of a victim or witness, it is "a course of conduct directed at a specific person that causes substantial emotional distress in such person and serves no legitimate purpose" (Black, 1991).

Limited public forum. See definition of "forum."

Manner. A way, mode, method of doing anything or mode of proceeding in any case or situation (Black, 1991).

Narrow tailoring (of a content-neutral restriction on the time, place, or manner of speech in a designated public forum). Being only as broad as is reasonably necessary to promote a substantial governmental interest that would be achieved less effectively without the restriction; no broader than absolutely necessary (Black, 1999).

A regulation of expression meets the narrow tailoring standard if the policy or regulation does not burden more speech than is necessary to further the government's level of interest as required by the type of scrutiny applied. See "strict scrutiny" or "rational basis."

Neutral principles. *Constitutional law*. Rules grounded in law, as opposed to rules based on personal interest or beliefs. In this context, the phrase was popularized by Herbert Wechsler. See *Toward Neutral Principles of Constitutional Law, 73* Harv. L. Rev. 1,1 959 (Black, 1999). When applied to restrictions of expression, those restrictions cannot be based in any way upon the content of the expression or the nature of the message to be delivered.

Obscenity. The character or quality of being obscene; conduct tending to corrupt the public morals by its indecency or lewdness (Black, 1991).

Although obscenity may be an unprotected form of expression, the courts apply obscenity in relation to the community standards of the specific community in question in a legal challenge. These standards are difficult to interpret and enforce and generally restrictive speech codes will not support an obscenity restriction. The U.S. Supreme Court, in *Miller v. California*, established a three-part test for obscenity. This test stated that the Constitution will not protect speech and expression that:

1. Taken as a whole, would be found by an average person to appeal to the prurient interests, when "community standards" are applied

2. Depicts or describes, in a patently offensive way, sexual conduct specifically defined by state law

3. Taken as a whole, lacks serious literary, artistic, political, or scientific merit

Overbreadth doctrine. *Constitutional law.* The doctrine holding that if a statute is so broadly written that it deters free expression, then it can be struck down on its face because of its chilling effect—even if it also prohibits acts that may legitimately be forbidden. The Supreme Court has used this doctrine to invalidate a number of laws, including those that would disallow peaceful picketing or require loyalty oaths (Black, 1999). See "vagueness doctrine."

Place, n. This word is a very indefinite term. It is applied to any locality, limited by boundaries, however large or however small. It may be used to designate a country, state, county, town, or a very small portion of a town. The extent of the locality designated by it must generally be determined by the connection in which it is used. In its primary and most general sense, it means locality, situation, or site, and it is also used to designate an occupied situation or building (Black, 1991).

Prior restraint. A system of prior restraint is any scheme that gives public officials the power to deny use of a forum in advance of its actual expression.

Any system of prior restraints of expression bears a heavy presumption against its constitutional validity, and the government carries a heavy burden of showing justification for imposition of such a restraint (Black, 1991).

Use of a prior restraint is any regulation that vests an administrative official with discretionary power to control, in advance, the use of a public forum for First Amendment activities. Prior restraint is not per-se unconstitutional, but it must be carefully scrutinized to guard against the unreasonable curtailment of free expression.

Public forum. *Constitutional law*. See definition for "forum."

Quid pro quo. What for what; something for something. Used in law for the giving of one valuable thing for another. It is nothing more than the mutual consideration that passes between the parties to a contract and which renders it valid and binding (Black, 1991).

Rational basis. The rational basis test is the lowest level of scrutiny applied to the governmental entity in determining if a law or policy violates an individual's or group's First Amendment right. Under this standard, a law will be upheld if it is rationally related to a legitimate interest. It is an easy standard for the governmental entity to meet, so most policies or rules examined under this standard are generally upheld unless they are arbitrary or irrational. Under this standard, the policy or rule **is presumed valid** and the individual or group would have the burden to prove that it was not valid.

Strict scrutiny. This is the level of standard a court will apply when a fundamental right, such as those created by the First Amendment, is involved. Under the strict scrutiny test, a law will be upheld only if it is necessary to achieve a compelling or overriding governmental interest. The court will always look to see if there are less burdensome means to accomplish the same purpose.

This is a very high level of scrutiny to meet, and the burden is on the governmental entity to prove that its law or policy is necessary to achieve the compelling interest. The court will not uphold a law or policy that burdens more people or more expression than is necessary to support the compelling interest. See also "compelling state interest test."

Strict scrutiny. To withstand strict scrutiny, a law must be in furtherance of a compelling government interest and go no further than necessary in impeding First Amendment rights. This rigorous test is only applied when there is a substantial interference with First Amendment rights (First Amendment Center glossary).

Symbolic speech A person's conduct that expresses opinions or thoughts about a subject and that may or may not be protected by the First Amendment. Actions which have as their primary purpose the expression of ideas as in the case of students who wore black arm bands to protest the war in Vietnam (Black, 1991).

Traditional public forum. See *forum*.

Time. The measure of duration. The word is expressive both of a precise *point* or *terminus* and of an *interval* between two points. A point in or space of duration at or during which some fact is alleged to have been committed (Black, 1991).

Vagueness. Uncertain breadth of meaning (the phrase "within a reasonable time" is plagued by vagueness—what is reasonable?). Though common in writings generally, vagueness raises due-process concerns if legislation does not provide fair notice of what is required or prohibited, so that enforcement might well become arbitrary (Black, 1999).

Vagueness doctrine. *Constitutional law*. The doctrine—based on the due process clause—requiring that a criminal statute state explicitly and definitely what acts are prohibited, so as to provide fair warning and preclude arbitrary enforcement. Also termed void-for-vagueness doctrine (Black, 1999).

Under this principle, a law or policy which does not fairly inform a person of what is commanded or prohibited is unconstitutional as violation of due process. The doctrine originates in the due process clause of the Fourteenth Amendment and is the basis for striking down legislation that contains insufficient warning of what conduct is unlawful (Black, 1991).

CHAPTER TWO

BIBLIOGRAPHY

Association for Student Judicial Affairs. (n.d.). *Circuit Representatives*. Retrieved July 25, 2006, from http://www.asjaonline. org/en/cms/?53

Black, H.G. (1991). *Black's Law Dictionary* (6th ed.). St. Paul, MN: West Publishing Company.

Black, H.G. (1999). *Black's Law Dictionary* (7th ed.). St. Paul, MN: West Publishing Company.

First Amendment Center. Online Glossary. Retrieved July 7, 2006 from http://www.firstamendmentcenter.org/about. aspx?item=glossary

Legal Encyclopedia [Electronic Version]. Retrieved July 7, 2006 from http://www.answers.com/library/Legal%20Encyclopedia

Weschler, Herbert. (1959). Toward Neutral Principles of Constitutional Law. *Harvard Law Review, 73*(1), 1-35.

CASES REFERENCED

Brandenburg v. Ohio, 395 U.S. 444 (1969)

Chaplinsky v. New Hampshire, 315 U.S. 568 (1942)

Miller v. California, 413 U.S. 15 (1973)

Sixteenth of September Planning Committee, Inc. v. City and County of Denver, Colorado, 474 F. Supp. 1333 (D.C. Colo. 1979)

Whitney v. California, 274 U.S. 357, 377 (1927)

CHAPTER THREE

Public And Private Institutions: What Are The Differences When Examining Free Speech?

"Freedom to differ is not limited to things that do not matter much. That would be a mere shadow of freedom. The test of its substance is the right to differ as to things that touch the heart of the existing order."

Justice Robert H. Jackson

CHAPTER THREE

Generally, the prohibitions on restricting free expression are limited to public colleges and universities. This is because, as a public entity, these institutions are considered to be "acting under color of the government" and thus are governed by the same type of limitations as created by the U.S. Constitution and subsequent legislation and common law as all other governmental entities, such as states and municipalities. Students enrolled at public institutions have constitutionally protected rights in addition to the specified rights articulated in college policies, codes, and handbooks, which provide contract rights to the students. For the most part, private institutions of higher education do not have the same type of restrictions created by governmental standards as do public institutions. Generally, the relationship of private institutions to their students is created exclusively by the language of the documents that create the contract between the student and the institution. There are exceptions to this general premise, however. Some states have created laws that impose a form of due process or other governmental-type restrictions on students enrolled at their private institutions. In addition, private institutions that have a substantial amount of federal funding for their institution through student financial aid and/or federal programs or grant dollars may be more vulnerable to challenge if they have a substantial enough "nexus" with the government to be subject to governmental restrictions. Thus, even private institutions should develop rules and policies that are not unreasonably restrictive or do not impose arbitrary limitations.

Keeping abreast of legal mandates, best practices, changing case law, and deep-rooted philosophical mindsets and beliefs are just a partial list of hurdles to navigate. Additionally, practitioners are often overwhelmed with the barrage of free speech claims when considering the Internet, expressive art forms, campus speakers, protests, and academic freedoms. Embracing the variety of First Amendment influences while considering different types of college campuses is certainly an undertaking. In many cases, it is the knowledgeable college and university administrator (often a well-informed judicial officer) that directs discussions regarding these free-speech matters to a positive outcome.

While there are certainly variations between public, private, and private religious institutions, what does this really mean for campus practitioners when examining differences between these types of colleges and why is it important?

> The First Amendment of the Constitution of the United States protects individual freedoms from *government* interference. It does not, as a rule, protect individual freedoms from interference by *private* organizations, such as corporations or private universities...private universities, then, are free, within the law, to define their own missions, and some choose to restrict academic freedom on behalf of this or that religious or particular agenda. (French, Lukianoff, and Silverglate, 2005, p. 49-50)

In "Free Speech and Colleges: An Interview with Paul McMasters," (Wallace-Wells, 1998), McMasters stated:

> "Public universities, of course, are subject to freedom of speech in the same way that any governmental or public institution is. They are required to protect freedom of speech and freedom of association and all other constitutional freedoms guaranteed by federal and local laws, and the courts have upheld that requirement." McMasters, responding to the Dartmouth speech code debate, goes on to state that private colleges are not governmental organs and "can, unfortunately, pretty much

do as they please." McMasters does capture the essence of this private school debate by highlighting the dichotomy of students' individual rights versus the college's set of rights. Basically, private colleges "operate under the law of contracts rather than constitutional law. Consequently, unless a private school specifically promises in its student handbook to provide free expression, it is under no obligation to do so." (p. 1)

PUBLIC-PRIVATE PARALLELS

Within the public-private dichotomy debate is another term known as "the state action doctrine." State action is a doctrine of constitutional law that imposes constitutional obligations upon private entities that somehow act in the place of the state.

Courts and commentators have dissected the state action concept in many different ways, but three approaches have emerged for attributing state action to an ostensibly private entity. When the private entity:

1. Acts as an agent of government in performing a particular task delegated to it by government (the delegated power theory) (see *Powe v. Miles, Wahba v. New York University, Greenya v. George Washington University*)

2. Performs a function that is generally considered the responsibility of government (the public function theory) (see *State v. Schmid*)

3. Obtains substantial resources, prestige, or encouragement from its involvement with government (the government contracts theory), its actions may become state action

subject to constitutional constraints (see *Burton V. Wilmington Parking Authority*, *Jackson v. Metropolitan Edison Co.*)

"Since the early 1970s, however, the trend of the U.S. Supreme Court's opinions has been to trim back the state action concept, making it less likely that courts will find state action to exist in particular cases. The leading case in this line involving educational institutions is *Rendell-Baker v. Kohn*, 457 U.S. 830 (1982)." (Kaplan & Lee, 1995, p. 47)

Another common argument is that free speech applications should follow federal money. Popular avenues of thought here usually center on federal funding for research and financial aid. According to McMasters (Wallace-Wells, 1998), "The courts haven't agreed on this argument." FIRE opined:

There are many students, faculty members, and even lawyers who believe, wholly erroneously, that if a college receives *any* federal or state funding it is therefore "public." In fact, accepting governmental funds usually makes the university subject only to the conditions—sometimes broad, sometimes narrow—explicitly attached to those specific programs to which the public funds are directed. (French, Lukianoff & Silverglate, 2005, p. 58)

Consider a similar narrowly tailored argument regarding how a different financing issue affects private institutions.

The Establishment Clause of the First Amendment of the U.S. Constitution prohibits Congress from making any law respecting an establishment of religion. It has been construed by the U.S. Supreme Court as prohibiting direct financial assistance by government

45

agencies to religious schools and colleges. In 1997, the Court decided *Agostini v. Felton*, 521 U.S. 203, 117 S.Ct. 1997, 138 L.Ed.2d 391 (1997), an important private school finance case in which the Court abandoned the presumption that the presence of public employees on parochial school grounds creates a symbolic union between church and state that violates the Establishment Clause. Under *Agostini*, government assistance to private schools must not result in government indoctrination or endorsement of religion. The recipients of government assistance must not be defined by reference to their religion, and the assistance must not create excessive entanglement between church and state. (*Higher Education Law in America*, 2002, p. 403)

For the campus practitioner, a more common-sense approach to how private schools should respond to free speech thought is found in its own printed materials. Simply stated, administrators should follow campus printed documents and adhere to the promises made. FIRE, rightfully so, is concerned about "bait-and-switch" practices where a particular promise is advertised but a different product is offered. The authors wrote:

> ...Private universities are obliged in some manner to adhere at least broadly to promises they make to incoming students about what kinds of institutions they are. [In summary,] the strength of that legal refuge depends on many factors:

★   the laws of the individual state in which the university is located;

★ the promises made or implied by university brochures, cata-
logues, handbooks, and disciplinary rules; and

★ the precise governance and funding of the institution. (French,
et al., 2005, p. 52)

In closing, there are pieces of legislation that should not be ignored when considering legal implications for the private college and
university. For example, California Education Code 94367, sometimes
known as "The Leonard Law," highlights a culmination of directives
for the public, private secular, and private religious institutions within
that state. While limited to California, this legislation does provide
insights that may guide the public-private dichotomy. For example, the
code states that "no private postsecondary educational institution shall
make or enforce any rule subjecting any student to disciplinary sanctions solely on the basis of conduct that is speech or other communication that, when engaged in outside the campus or facility of a private
postsecondary institution, is protected from governmental restriction
by the First Amendment to the United States Constitution or Section 2 of Article 1 of the California Constitution." Also, the legislation
provides guidance for the private postsecondary educational institution
"that is controlled by a religious organization, to the extent that the
application of this section would not be consistent with the religious
tenets of the organization."

Understanding the foundation of the public-private dichotomy
provides knowledge, instruction, and practical application. To ensure
free speech as a precious right and privilege, it is essential to embrace
the many facets of the First Amendment in the broadest sense and be
informed enough to guide others through specific details and circumstances. Regardless of whether the institution is public, private-secular,

or private-religious, the freedoms we enjoy must not be taken for granted. Administrators and institutions of higher education must continue to provide academic excellence in an environment that is conducive to free expression.

BIBLIOGRAPHY

California Education Code 94367 [Electronic Version]. Retrieved July 7, 2006 from http://caselaw.lp.findlaw.com/cacodes/edc/94367.html

French, D., Lukianoff, G., & Silverglate, H. (2005). *FIRE's Guide to Free Speech on Campus*. Philadelphia, PA: Foundation for Individual Rights in Education.

Higher Education Law in America (3rd ed.). (2002). Birmingham, AL: Oakstone Legal and Business Publications

Kaplan, W.A. & Lee, B.A. (1995). *The Law in Higher Education: A Comprehensive Guide to Legal Implications of Administrative Decision Making* (3rd ed). San Francisco, CA: Jossey-Bass Publishers.

Wallace-Wells, B. (1998, Nov. 10). Free Speech and Colleges: An Interview with Paul McMasters [Electronic Version]. *The Dartmouth Review*. Retrieved July 6, 2006 from http://www.dartreview.com/archives/1998/11/10/free_speech_and_colleges_an_interview_with_paul_mcmasters.php

CASES REFERENCED

Agostini v. Felton, 521 U.S. 203, 117 S.Ct. 1997, 136 L.Ed.2d 391 (1997)

Burton v. Wilmington Parking Authority, 365 U.S. 715, 722 (1961)

Greenya v. George Washington University, 512 F.2d 556 (D.C. Cir. 1975)

Jackson v. Metropolitan Edison Co., 419 U.S. 345, 351 (1974)

Powe v. Miles, 407 F.2d 73 (2d Cir. 1968)

Rendell-Baker v. Kohn, 457 U.S. 830 (1982)

49

CHAPTER THREE

State v. Schmid, 84 N. J. 535 (N. J., 1980)

Wahba v. New York University, 492 F.2d 96 (2d Cir 1974)

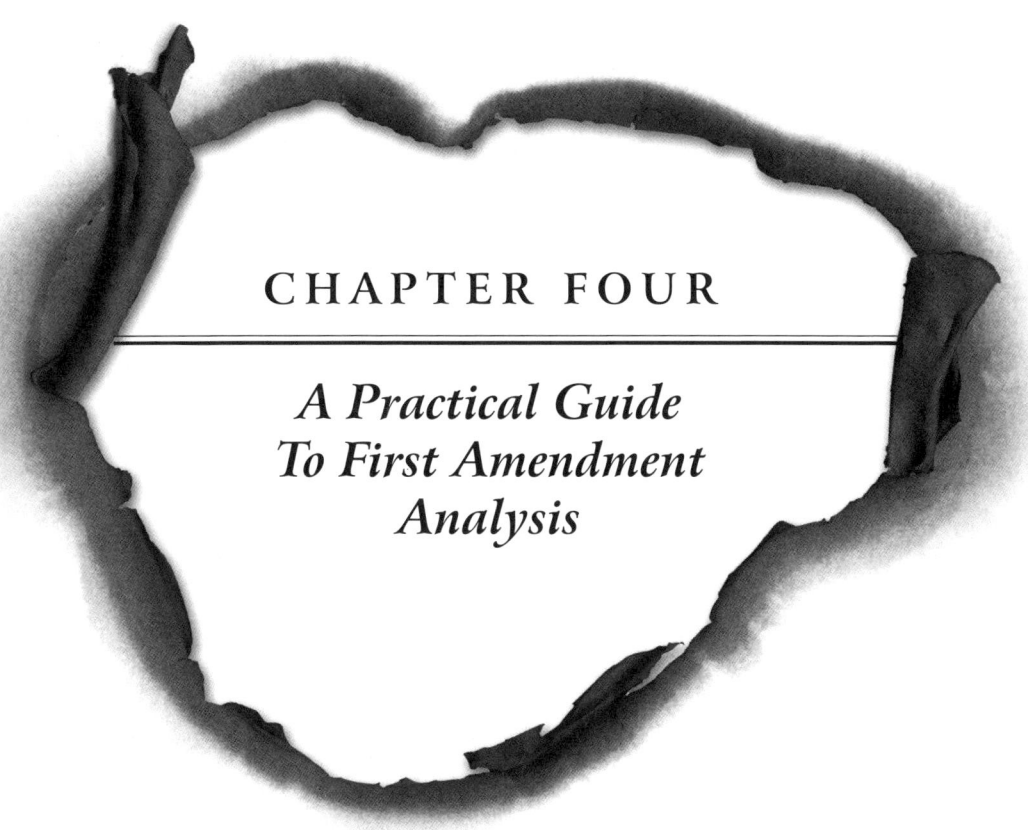

CHAPTER FOUR

A Practical Guide To First Amendment Analysis

"I have always been among those who believed that the greatest freedom of speech was the greatest safety, because if a man is a fool the best thing to do is to encourage him to advertise the fact by speaking."

President Woodrow Wilson

CHAPTER FOUR

As the examples in this book demonstrate, college and university administrators continually face challenges regarding the First Amendment. Regulation of conduct as well as expression may fall under First Amendment restrictions if the content of the conduct is the primary issue at hand. The courts are likely to uphold regulation of conduct that is not exclusively based upon expression. First Amendment challenges based on freedom of expression include expression through speech and writing, campus policies related to access, and guidelines limiting the use of space on a public campus.

These may all involve difficult decisions for administrators. Even determining what constitutes "expression" can present a challenge.

> Freedom of speech is not limited to spoken words alone, but includes several types of speech. Pure speech involves only spoken words, such as debates and public meetings, and has the greatest protection under the First Amendment. Speech-plus is speech combined with action, such as demonstrations and picketing. The speech portion of the speech-plus is generally protected, but the action portion may be regulated.
>
> Symbolic speech is conduct that conveys a message in itself, without spoken words, and is sometimes known as expressive conduct. (Monk, 1991, p. 62-63)

Although the courts generally recognize that the First Amendment provides substantial protection for free expression, it does not guarantee unfettered access to property simply because it is owned or controlled by a government entity (*Perry Educ. Ass'n. v. Perry Local Educators' Ass'n.*). Thus, although courts give priority to the protection of freedom of expression, public institutions have the right to impose reasonable regulations compatible with their mission by applying a careful analysis of the content, the forum, and the effect of the expression.

The most difficult question the Supreme Court faces in First Amendment cases is whether the citizen or the state bears the burden of persuasion. The answer to this question will most often decide the outcome. Over the years, the Court has vacillated between two tests. One stresses "the preferred place be given in our scheme to the...indispensable democratic freedoms secured by the First Amendment." Under this "preferred position" test, government officials must prove a "compelling" reason for laws that restrict free expression. Governments usually fail this stringent test. The alternate test is much easier to pass. This "involves a balancing by the courts of the competing interests at stake" in this case. The "balancing" test places the government's heavy thumb on the scales of justice. Laws judged by this test rarely fail to pass.

The Supreme Court has shifted over the years between the "preferred position" and "balancing" tests in First Amendment cases. In more than a thousand cases decided between 1942 and 1973, the Court has generally upheld the rights of individuals against governmental restrictions. But the Justices have consistently applied another test to the challenged laws. The "time place and manner" test allows reasonable restrictions on free expression to protect the public. Under this test people can voice their opinions in streets and parks, but not in residential neighborhoods at 3:00 AM. They can picket abortion clinics, but they cannot block access to

> patients. They can use loud speakers, but not above rea-
> sonable decibel levels. Applying this test has not been
> easy, but the Court has generally allowed protest that
> takes place in a "public forum" and that does not dis-
> rupt the peace and quiet of residential areas. (Irons &
> Guitton, 1993, p. 59)

College and university administrators, particularly those at public institutions, seek concrete guidance to analyze First Amendment challenges on their campuses in order to support the mission of their institution, encourage the free exchange of ideas, limit disruptive activity, and reduce their risk of legal challenge (not **eliminate** legal risk). There is no "bright line" that can be applied to provide absolute protection or give the "correct response" for each situation. However, conducting a First Amendment analysis of the forum in which the regulation will occur (in order to develop legally sound policies and an appropriate response protocol) is essential in order to provide a response that meets the academic mission of the institution and creates an acceptable level of legal risk. Administrators should document, in writing, the basis for decisions at each step of this process. The following guidelines provide a threshold approach to such analysis.

THRESHOLD ANALYSIS

Step One: Identifying First Amendment Issues

The first step is to determine if the issue presented includes First Amendment implications. This may seem obvious to some, but many First Amendment issues that administrators face on campus come carefully disguised. Therefore, the following should be considered.

★ Are there any components of "expression" in the activity in question? Such expression may include requests to speak in various locations on campus; leafleting; articles or advertisements in the campus newspaper; notices or statements on sidewalks, bulletin boards, clothing and messages affixed thereto; kiosks; notices on residence hall doors; communication via the campus computing system; accessing Internet sites from the campus computing system; plays, skits, or other public productions.

★ Does the issue at hand have any religious components?

★ Does it involve content in the campus newspaper or on radio or television stations?

★ Does it involve a group activity on campus, such as a demonstration, protest, walkout, or rally?

★ Does it involve a request for a meeting room?

★ Does it involve any restrictions on a group or organization or affiliation?

★ Does it involve recognition or financial support for student organizations?

If any of the answers are yes, then the issue is likely one that demands First Amendment review.

Step Two: Exceptions to First Amendment Protection

If there are First Amendment issues to consider, the next step is to identify if any clear exceptions to First Amendment protection apply.

While there **are** specific exceptions, each one requires careful analysis of the college's or university's particular set of facts. Courts will apply the exceptions "narrowly," which means that if there is a question about whether the exception should apply, it will not apply unless there is substantial evidence to support the exception. General exceptions include:

★ **Defamation (libel, slander):** These oral or written falsehoods [not a statement of opinion] are communicated to third parties and would harm another's reputation.

★ **Obscenity:** This is legally defined as when the description or depiction of sexual conduct, taken as a whole, by the average person, applying contemporary community standards, portrays sex in a patently offensive way; appeals to the prurient interests of individuals, and, when taken as a whole, lacks serious literary, artistic, political, or scientific value.

★ **Disruption of the academic environment:** This expression substantially infringes on reasonable campus rules, interrupts classes, or substantially interferes with the opportunity of other students to obtain an education.

★ **True threat of violence:** This exception applies to a serious expression of an intent to harm.

★ **Behavior directed to inciting or producing an imminent lawless action:** This speech must present a clear, present, and immediately imminent threat before it can be prohibited.

★ **Fighting words:** This exception must be used with extreme caution, as the courts generally won't support limitations based on this exception unless the expression, "Which by its very utterance inflicts injury or tends to incite an immediate breach of the peace," can be applied.

★ **Invasion of privacy:** College administrators seldom encounter this exception, which applies to the right of individuals not to be subject to unwanted speech in their own homes; it could, however, be applicable in residence hall rooms.

★ **Sexual or racial (or other discriminatory) harassment:** This applies only when the expression is "sufficiently severe or pervasive to deny or limit a student's ability to participate in or benefit from the educational program." It must be something beyond the expression of views, words, symbols, or thoughts that some person finds merely offensive.

If one of the above exceptions clearly applies, and the supporting facts are documented, then the college or university may limit, restrict, or turn down the request, or take action to discipline the behavior, but it must also take into consideration the following elements:

★ That the regulation must not create an impermissible prior restraint (see the definition section in Chapter Two)

★ Should not burden more expression than necessary to fulfill the purpose for the regulation

★ Should not create a "chilling effect"(see the definition section in Chapter Two) on the expression

★ Should not create unfettered discretion for control by the campus administration

★ Should not be so vague or ambiguous that it fails to provide sufficient notice of what expression will be limited

It is important to remember that if an administrator makes the determination that an exception applies, he or she must be prepared to support that said expression qualifies as an exception to free speech. If an exception does not clearly apply, then go to Step Three in the analysis.

Step Three: Forum Analysis

Selective limitations on expression, based on the content of the speech or expression, are generally always prohibited. That is, unless the expression involved one of the exceptions to the First Amendment (see Step Two), the administration may not prohibit it simply because it offends or is outrageous, hurtful, shocking, vulgar, rude, or offensive (or any of the other terms inconsistent with the ideal learning environment). The courts have clearly made a distinction here between a K–12 setting and a university setting regarding expression. Courts have upheld the restriction of vulgar or offensive speech in the K–12 setting, while they have stated that in the college setting "the mere dissemination of ideas, no matter how offensive to good taste, may not be shut off in the name alone of conventions of decency" (*Papish v. Board of Curators of the University of Missouri*). This would include so-called "hate" speech.

While a content-neutral, reasonable "time, place, or manner" limitation may be applied, administrators should never undertake even this level of limitation without further analysis. What is "reasonable" depends on the "forum" in which the First Amendment matter is occurring.

Public institutions are afforded a certain degree of latitude to control conduct on their campuses, however, the level of control exerted should be evaluated based upon the character of the location at issue. (Note: The use of the term "location" should be viewed as generic and applied to any type of First Amendment issue.) Public college campuses consist of several different kinds of "forums" and the First Amendment does not guarantee access to a location simply because it is owned by a public entity. If the institution is going to restrict or discipline a First Amendment activity, there must be a balancing analysis applied between the interest of those seeking expressive activity and the institution's interest in prohibiting, limiting, or disciplining such activity.

The U.S. Supreme Court adopted a forum analysis to determine the degree of reasonable regulation that can be applied to content-neutral expression. Each of the forum terms are defined in Chapter Two of this book, so this discussion will focus on the practical use of the forum designation.

Traditional public forums and **designated public forums** are generally subject to the same degree of analysis and standards for limiting expression. Traditional public forums are those that, by tradition, are entrusted for use by the public, such as public sidewalks, streets, and parks. Designated public forums have the same degree of "rights" as traditional public forums, but these are the areas on campus **specifically assigned** by the public institution to serve as public forums, such as "free speech zones," the mall, gazebos, and green space. This type of forum does not occur by default; **rather it must be specifically designated**. A designated public forum does not have to remain designated as such forever, rather the space may be reassigned (with appropriate notice) to a different designation. The degree of restriction that may be applied to traditional public and designated public forums is the least restrictive of all. It is very difficult to restrict speech in either of these public forums. These two forums are subject to what the courts call a "strict scrutiny" standard. That is, the institution must be able to articulate a "compelling interest" in limiting expression and the limitation imposed must be "narrowly tailored" to achieve that goal. For a public institution, this means that there is an automatic assumption that expression **may not be restricted** and the institution has to overcome that assumption by articulating the legitimate reason or pedagogical interest that **should allow** the administration to restrict or prohibit the speech. Examples would include protecting the educational environment of its students in support of the institutional mission or ensuring public safety. The "narrowly tailored" term means that the restrictions the institution imposes address only that stated legitimate reason or interest and not other forms of expression ("...does not burden substantially more speech than is necessary to further the stated legitimate [compelling] government interest").

The college or university must also be able to demonstrate that there are other avenues available on campus to communicate the same expression and that the limitations are applied evenly to everyone. Outside of specific public safety and disruption of the environment justifications, courts do not often find administrative regulation in these forums to meet the compelling interest test. Students distributing literature in a pedestrian crosswalk, requiring vehicles to swerve around them, could constitute a legitimate public safety concern. A large number of students gathered in the mall area to listen to a speaker would not rise to this level, even if administrators grow uneasy due to the size of the burgeoning crowd. A legitimate concern related to disruption of the campus environment might occur when megaphones are used immediately outside of a classroom while class is in session. Students and faculty who are in an administrator's office to complain bitterly about the campus preacher on the mall whose message upsets the crowd do not represent a legitimate reason for limiting the preacher's speech, even if such speech upsets those hearing it. Simply being upset is not the same as a disruption to the campus environment. Such a distinction is not always an easy one to make. As Gary Pavela noted, even college administrators dealing with protests and rallies in the 1960s failed "...to distinguish between dissent and disruption. The former is (or should be) a welcome part of campus life. The latter strikes at the heart of the university as a place where diverse points of view can be expressed fearlessly and passionately—but without physical coercion" (Pavela, 2006, p. 1).

In the same *Law and Policy Report*, Pavela cites *Dissent and Disruption*, a 1971 Carnegie Commission Report, which made the fundamental distinction: "We define it as dissent if no one is injured, threatened or abused; no property is stolen or damaged; no important activities are impeded; no crimes are committed or campus rules broken; and ingress and egress are not hindered" (Pavela, p. 1).

The next forum is the **limited public forum** (also known as a **designated limited public forum**). These locations are typically ones the institution has opened for expressive activity but only for a content-neutral limited purpose. For example, they may only be used by student or faculty groups or are limited to campaign speeches for student government association candidates. Typically, if a location serves more than one purpose, the institution could state that it gives priority to one type of expression over another. For example, a campus auditorium may give priority to theater productions.

Limitations placed on expressive activity in limited public forums must be governed by a written use policy that includes the stated purpose of the location and any limitations, and there must be consistent enforcement of the policy. In this type of forum, the regulation on expression may be more strict and the standard applied is one of "reasonableness." That is, if the limitations imposed on the expressive activity are consistent with the purpose of the location, college mission, or historical use, they are likely to meet the reasonableness test. However, this type of forum also requires that the policies or prohibitions limiting expression are narrowly tailored and do not restrict more expression than is essential to achieve the purpose of the policy. In this type of forum, the courts generally will support the institution giving priority to college entities over non-college entities as long as the priority is consistently applied. Even if the institution did not select the **most** reasonable means of regulation, courts may uphold it if there is a clearly stated reason for the restriction.

Finally, public institutions maintain areas that are considered non-public forum areas, which would include campus offices, residence hall rooms, and classrooms. If the expression in question is incompatible with the purpose of the location, that expression may be limited. In this forum location, the limitations on expression are given the most latitude. The institution may impose more limitations on expressive activity as long as those limitations are reasonable in nature and do not limit expression simply because of the content or viewpoint expressed. The reasonableness of the restriction is reviewed in light of both the purpose and nature of the location as well as surrounding circumstances.

Courts have consistently held that although public colleges and universities are not entirely public forums, neither can they identify themselves as completely non-public or limited public forums in nature. To the extent that a campus has park areas, sidewalks, streets, or other similar common areas, these areas are public forums, at least for the students, regardless of whether the institution has so designated them. To allow greater regulation would permit institutional control over casual conversations or other non-disruptive casual activity (*Roberts v. Haragan*). Therefore, each institution must identify those areas that constitute each type of forum and ensure that any regulations or limitations are consistent with the type of location involved.

To summarize, the notion that administrators can freely implement "reasonable time, place, and manner" regulations is misleading, because only in two of the four forums—the limited public forum and the non-public forum—are these regulations easily applied. In the traditional public forum and the designated public forum, "time, place, and manner" restrictions are subject to the strict scrutiny test.

Readers are encouraged not to oversimplify the complexity of the First Amendment. While a chart may be helpful for visual learners, the authors can not state firmly enough that there are no absolutes. The charts reflect general guidelines, a starting place for discussion and further analysis.

FORUM ANALYSIS CHART

TYPE OF FORUM	DEFINITION	COMMON CAMPUS EXAMPLES	DEGREE OF REGULATION POSSIBLE
Traditional Public Forum	Places which by long tradition or by governmental default have been devoted to assembly or debate	Campus mall, public streets through campus, public sidewalks	Content-neutral time, place, and manner limitations may be placed on expression, however, the limitation is subject to a strict scrutiny standard. Therefore, any limitation must serve a compelling government interest; be narrowly tailored so the limitation does not burden more expression than necessary to meet the compelling interest; and leave open ample alternative channels of communication.
Designated Public Forum	Areas on campus specifically assigned by the institution to serve as public forum location	Designated "free speech" zones such as gazebos, green space, campus mall areas, main walkways through campus	Content-neutral time, place, and manner limitations may be placed on expression; however, the limitation is subject to a strict scrutiny standard. Therefore, any limitation must serve a compelling government interest; be narrowly tailored so the limitation does not burden more expression than necessary to meet the compelling interest; and leave open ample alternative channels of communication.

TYPE OF FORUM	DEFINITION	COMMON CAMPUS EXAMPLES	DEGREE OF REGULATION POSSIBLE
Limited Public Forum	Locations that the institution has opened for expressive activity with a content-neutral limited purpose	Auditoriums, meeting rooms that may be made available at times to non-college groups, athletic facilities during events	Limitations must be governed by a written-use policy that includes the stated purpose of the location and any limitations, and the limitations must be enforced consistently. Regulation may be more strict and must only be reasonable and viewpoint-neutral. Policies limiting expression must be narrowly tailored and must not restrict more expression than is necessary to achieve the interest. Institutions may give priority for space to college groups over non-college groups.
Nonpublic Forum	Locations that have not, by tradition or designation, been open to the general public	Classrooms, campus offices, residence hall rooms	If the expression in question is incompatible with the purpose of the location, that expression may be limited. Expression may not be limited simply because of the content or viewpoint expressed. Regulation takes into account the purpose and nature of the location as well as the circumstances.

This threshold approach to First Amendment analysis may be helpful when the college administrator is faced with the issue of responding to or limiting expression that may have Constitutional protection. It is important to recognize that conducting a forum analysis generally represents the beginning of an institution's approach to regulation of activity protected by the First Amendment. Any subsequent

65

regulation to limit activity, based upon the nature of the forum, must include consideration of other elements discussed at the end of Step Two that could trip up a college administrator. Therefore, the analysis and development of regulations limiting expression should occur in collaboration with appropriate college/university personnel, including campus legal counsel if possible, and should be accompanied by careful documentation.

UNPROTECTED SPEECH

This chart provides an overview of various forms of expression that may not enjoy First Amendment protection, as discussed earlier in this chapter. Each is discussed briefly with a definition and accompanying criteria for determining when the concept is applicable. The use of a chart is not meant to oversimplify the complexity of this evaluation. Administrators are strongly encouraged to consult with legal counsel regarding the specific circumstances of any incident on campus

CONCERN	TESTS	KEY RESOURCE
Sexual Harassment	Unwelcome speech or conduct of a sexual nature that is so serious (i.e., severe, persistent, or pervasive) as to deny or limit a student's ability to participate in or benefit from the educational program. This conduct must be evaluated from the perspective of a reasonable person in the alleged victim's position, considering all the circumstances, including the alleged victim's age. This determination requires an analysis of the totality of the circumstances.	*Revised Sexual Harassment Guidance, U.S. Dept. of Ed., Office for Civil Rights* (2001) Title IX case law *Gebser* and *Davis* cases

CONCERN	TESTS	KEY RESOURCE
Racial Harassment	Unwelcome speech or conduct based on a person's race, color, or national origin that is so serious (i.e., severe, persistent, pervasive) as to deny or limit a student's ability to participate in or benefit from the educational program. This conduct must be evaluated from the perspective of a reasonable person in the alleged victim's position, considering all the circumstances, including the alleged victim's age and race.	U.S. Dept. of Ed., Office for Civil Rights Guidelines Title VI
Obscenity	Miller Test: a. Whether the average person applying contemporary community standards would find the work, taken as a whole, appeals to prurient interests b. Whether the work depicts or describes sexual conduct, as outlined in state law, in a patently offensive way c. Whether the work as a whole lacks serious literary, artistic, political, or scientific value	Justice Berger from *Miller v. California*
Fighting Words	Chaplinsky Test: Use of insulting "fighting words," which, by their very utterance, inflict injury or tend to incite an immediate breach of the peace. At present, the "fighting words" doctrine is probably limited to provocative, face-to-face encounters that might also be treated as physical threats or intimidation. (Pavela, 2004, p. 3215)	*Chaplinsky v. New Hampshire*
Incitement of Imminent Lawless Action (such as burning a classroom building)	Brandenburg Test: In order for the government to intervene, the speaker must: a. Subjectively intend incitement (imminent evil) b. Use words which are likely to produce action (imminent action) c. Openly encourage or urge incitement	*Brandenburg v. Ohio*

CONCERN	TESTS	KEY RESOURCE
True Threat	Intimidation in the constitutionally pro-scribable sense of the word is a type of true threat, where a speaker directs a threat to a person or group of persons with the intent of placing the victim in fear of bodily harm or death. The intent in this language is to protect a victim from the fear of violence and does not rely on the speaker's plan to carry out the threat.	*Virginia v. Black*
	A statement which, in the entire context and under all the circumstances, a rea-sonable person would foresee would be interpreted by those to whom the statement is communicated as a serious expression of intent to inflict bodily harm upon that person.	*Planned Parenthood v. American Coalition of Life Activists*
Defamation (Libel)	*New York Times* Test: Prohibits a public official from recovering damages for a defamatory falsehood relating to official conduct unless proven that the statement was made with "actual malice," that is: 1. with knowledge that it was false or 2. with reckless disregard of whether it was false or not.	*New York Times v. Sul-livan*
	Hustler Test (satire of public officials or figures): Public officials and public figures in general must prove actual malice or intentional infliction of emotional distress, even when no damage is done to reputation. The test is whether a parody, cartoon, or something clearly for entertainment purposes is outra-geous in its intent.	*Hustler Magazine v. Falwell*

CONCERN	TESTS	KEY RESOURCE
Internet Defamation	On the modern college campus, defamatory statements are often expressed electronically via blogs, Web pages and e-mail. Even though this forum may be less traditional than the Sullivan Test intended, no new definitions or tests have yet surfaced that are specific to electronic defamation.	

BIBLIOGRAPHY

Irons, P. & Guitton, S. (Eds.). (1993). *May It Please the Court*. New York, NY: The New Press.

Monk, L.R. (1991). *The Bill of Rights: A User's Guide*. Alexandria, VA. Close Up Publishing.

Office for Civil Rights, Department of Education. (2001). *Revised Sexual Harassment Guidance: Harassment of Student by School Employees, Other Students or Third Parties* [Electronic Version]. Retrieved July 7, 2006 from http://www.ed.gov/legislation/FedRegister/other/2001-1/011901b.html

Office for Civil Rights, Department of Education. (2006). Education and Title VI. http://www.ed.gov/about/offices/list/ocr/docs/hq43e4.html

Pavela, G. (2004, Jan. 26). Lawful Limits on Freedom of Expression, Synfax Weekly Report. (Available from College Administration Publications, Inc, 830-D Fairview Road, Asheville, NC 28803-1081)

Pavela, G. (2006, April 24). ASJA Law and Policy Report. Number 215. [Electronic Version]. Retrieved July 7, 2006 from http://www.asjaonline.org/

CASES REFERENCED

Brandenburg v. Ohio, 395 U.S. 444 (1969).

Chaplinsky v. New Hampshire, 315 U.S. 568 (1942)

Davis v. Monroe County Bd. of Educ., 526 U.S. 629 (1999)

Gebser v. Lago Vista Independent School District, 524 U.S. 274 (1998)

Hustler Magazine v. Falwell, 485 U.S. 46 (1988)

Miller v. California, 413 U.S. 15 (1973)

New York Times v. Sullivan, 376 U.S. 254 (1964)

Papish v. Board of Curators of the University of Missouri, 410 U.S. 667 (1973)

Perry Educ. Ass'n v. Perry Local Educators' Ass'n, 460 U.S. 37, 46 (1983)

Planned Parenthood v. American Coalition of Life Activists, 290 /f,3d 1058m (9th Cir. 2002)

Roberts v. Haragan, 346 F. Supp. 2d 853 (N.D. Tex. 2004)

Virginia v. Black, 538 U.S. 343 (2003)

CHAPTER FIVE

Campus Scenarios and Commentary

*"Those who profess to favor freedom, and
yet depreciate agitation, are men who want
rain without thunder or lightning."*

**Frederick Douglass,
American abolitionist and author**

CHAPTER FIVE

As we saw in Chapter One, the responsibilities of a college administrator often require a delicate balance of protecting the rights of
many different parties while maintaining a campus atmosphere conducive to learning.

This chapter presents numerous scenarios that deal with some
of the most common free-speech issues facing American colleges and
universities. It should be assumed that each incident takes place at a
public institution unless otherwise noted. Each scenario provides commentary that informs the reader of key legal concepts and is followed
by a series of questions to consider in the context of a specific college
or university. The reader may wish to go to Chapter Two to review the
definitions of these concepts. Throughout each scenario and commentary, references are made to relevant court cases. Brief summaries of
many of these cases can be found in Chapter Eight, offering the reader
a brief description of key facts of the case and a full citation for locat-
ing the case using Findlaw or similar Web resource guides.

SCENARIO 1. HATE SOLICITATION

After his night class, Dr. Carlisle finds a notice placed under
his car's windshield wiper, and those of other cars parked nearby,
advocating violence against African Americans. The picture on
the flier features rifle scope crosshairs superimposed on the head
of an African American man. Dr. Carlisle calls campus security
and demands that these offensive fliers be collected and de-
stroyed *immediately*.

Relevant Questions

1. Can the campus allow or prohibit such solicitation?

A campus parking lot would most likely be considered a non-public forum, if it has not, by tradition or designation, been open to the general public. This would be true if the institution controls access to the parking (e.g., parking passes are required or there is a gate arm). If, however, the lot has spaces for public parking of any kind or if the institution has designated or opened the parking lot for expressive activity (by encouraging or allowing leafleting or other forms of expression), then it would be considered a designated public forum which would be subject to a lesser degree of regulation.

Although the campus may prohibit such solicitation, any prohibition must serve a narrowly tailored government interest and that interest must outweigh the interest of free expression. In this particular instance, it might be argued that someone putting fliers on cars would be walking in and out of vehicle traffic lanes and would pose a safety hazard. Such regulation must also allow for ample alternative means to communicate the message on campus and must be done in a content-neutral manner. In practice, this means that staff may not approve or prohibit solicitation based on whether they agree or disagree with the content ideologically. The fact that the flier may hurt someone's feelings or anger a person passing by cannot be a determining factor in the application of the campus solicitation policy.

2. Can the fliers be removed and destroyed as requested?

No, unless campus policy prohibits all distribution of fliers in this parking lot and not just those that someone finds offensive.

Some campuses require, in their solicitation and leafleting policy, that individuals or groups wishing to post or distribute information provide their name and contact information on the request for a permit to canvass or solicit. Some campuses have required that the individual or organization provide a name and contact number on each flier distributed. In theory, if people take issue with what is said on the flier, they can go directly to the source and voice their concerns. The courts may determine that requiring the organization's name and contact information on every flier is too restrictive as shown recently in *Justice for All v. Faulkner*.

The judges in *Justice For All* found the following:

> The University of Texas at Austin ("the University") is the flagship campus of the University of Texas System. Justice For All ("JFA") is a student anti-abortion group at the University. JFA brought this action challenging the University's "Literature Policy," which requires that all printed materials distributed on campus bear the name of a university-affiliated person or organization responsible for their distribution. JFA contends that the policy is an unconstitutional restriction on anonymous speech in a designated public forum. The University responds that the policy is a reasonable, viewpoint-neutral regulation of speech within a limited public forum. The district court agreed with JFA and issued a permanent injunction barring enforcement of the Literature Policy to prevent JFA from engaging in anonymous leafleting.

> As a general proposition, anonymous speech is protected by the First Amendment. See, e.g., *McIntyre v. Ohio Elections Commission*, 514 U.S. 334 (1995); *Buckley*

v. American Constitutional Law Foundation, Inc., 525 U.S. 182, 199-200 (1999); *Talley v. California*, 362 U.S. 60, 64 (1960). In striking down prohibitions on anonymous publication, the Supreme Court has noted, inter alia, the importance of anonymity as a means of permitting "[p]ersecuted groups and sects" to "criticize oppressive practices and laws." *Talley*, 362 U.S. at 64.

More specifically, the First Amendment's protection of anonymous speech extends beyond traditional publishing to encompass anonymous leafleting. In *Talley*, for example, the Supreme Court held void a city ordinance barring the distribution of handbills that did not include the name and address of both the author and distributor. See id. at 60-61, 65. Moreover, the Court observed in McIntyre that "anonymous pamphleteering is not a pernicious, fraudulent practice, but an honorable tradition of advocacy and dissent," which "exemplifies the purpose behind the Bill of Rights, and of the First Amendment in particular." 514 U.S. at 357.

The University's case is based on a general assertion that "the University campus" is a limited public forum. The University suggests that to hold otherwise would render the entire campus "the equivalent of a public park," insofar as any regulation of speech by "students, teachers, or anyone else" would be subject to strict scrutiny. Moreover, the University notes that it affirmatively prohibits speech by "off-campus persons or organizations"—i.e., anyone who is not a student, faculty member, or staff member—and contends that the district court's order, if upheld, would undermine its ability to do so. The

University's arguments do not reflect an appreciation of the distinction between limited and designated public forums as they exist within the university property.

The distinction between limited and designated public forums is not a simple "all-or-nothing" proposition. The Supreme Court's forum analysis jurisprudence does not require us to choose between the polar extremes of treating an entire university campus as a forum designated for all types of speech by all speakers, or, alternatively, as a limited forum where any reasonable restriction on speech must be upheld. Instead, as the Supreme Court indicated in *Arkansas Public Television Assn. v. Forbes*, a given forum may be designated for one class of speaker or speech, and still "limited" with respect to others. See 523 U.S. 666, 677-81 (1998) ("If the government excludes a speaker who falls within the class to which a designated public forum is made generally available, its action is subject to strict scrutiny."). [Justice for All v. Faulkner, 410 F.3d 760 (5th Cir. 2005)]

3. Can the institution limit posting/solicitation/pamphleteering privileges to only recognized campus groups?

Yes; however, the language must be included in the campus policy and would have to be written in such as way as to tie the solicitation of the group to the educational mission (including co-curricular activities) of the institution. Having groups that wish to distribute materials identify themselves may be allowed, and this can be important to the institution so that groups are held responsible for abiding by posting and clean-up policies. As *Justice for All v. Faulkner* illustrated, however, there may be less restrictive ways of accomplishing this goal other than requiring the group's name to appear on the flier. Outside groups wishing to post may be required to be sponsored by a recognized student organization or university department so that there is still an on-campus responsible party.

4. Does the content of the flier reflect a "true threat," which would not have First Amendment privileges?

Typically, a true threat is measured by whether it communicates a serious intent to inflict harm, taking into consideration the context of the communication. Three court cases are especially instructive in this assessment.

In *Brandenburg v. Ohio*, the Supreme Court made it clear that the First Amendment protects speech that advocates violence but **not** speech that is directed to inciting or producing **imminent** lawless action and is likely to produce such action. In this case, a film of a Ku Klux Klan rally was broadcast that showed Klan members with weapons. One member claimed that "there might have to be some revengeance [sic] taken." As the oration did not incite or produce imminent lawless action, the speech was protected. The flier on Dr. Carlisle's car certainly advocates violence but it does not call in a specific way for imminent lawless action and does not appear likely to cause such.

In *Watts v. U.S.*, the Supreme Court took the context of the situation into account to determine if speech was mere political hyperbole as opposed to a true threat. In this case, a draft protester said, "If they ever make me carry a rifle, the first man I want to get in my sights is L.B.J." The Court determined that the context of an anti-draft rally rendered this a political statement rather than a true threat and was, thus, protected speech.

79

CHAPTER FIVE

In *Planned Parenthood v. American Coalition of Life Activists,* the Court determined that the context of a message, even though not explicitly stating a threat, stripped the message of its First Amendment protection. In this case, a pro-life group distributed "guilty" posters that contained the names, photos, and addresses of abortion providers and advocates. Although the posters did not state a direct threat, previous similar postings had preceded the murder of three people.

> ACLA was aware that a "wanted"-type poster would likely be interpreted as a serious threat of death or bodily harm by a doctor in the reproductive health services community who was identified on one, given the previous pattern of "WANTED" posters identifying a specific physician followed by that physician's murder. The same is true of the posting about these physicians on that part of the "Nuremberg Files" where lines were drawn through the names of doctors who provided abortion services and who had been killed or wounded. (*Planned Parenthood v. American Coalition of Life Activists*, 2002)

The Court defined a true threat as one in which "in the entire context, and under all the circumstances, a reasonable person would foresee would be interpreted by those to whom the statement is communicated as a serious expression of intent to inflict bodily harm upon that person." In Dr. Carlisle's situation, there are no extraneous circumstances presented that would cause a reasonable person to interpret the message as such an expression.

Additional Tips

★ The incident should be reported to security/campus police and the campus judicial officer.

★ Copies of any group's flier that purports violence may also be reported to the Southern Poverty Law Center and/or Tolerance.org, organizations that track hate groups.

SCENARIO 2. SEXUAL HARASSMENT BY E-MAIL

Allyson receives her 22nd message this week on her university e-mail while in the computer lab. The message suggests sexual acts that the sender would like to perform on her. Photos from *Hustler* magazine have been scanned into messages for added effect. Allyson asks the sender to stop e-mailing her messages. Allyson is so bothered by the messages that she quits going to the lab and her academic work suffers as a consequence. Before she leaves the lab, she reports the harassing e-mail to the lab monitor. The monitor is able to identify the sender and reports the complaint to the Affirmative Action Officer and the campus conduct officer. Brian, the author of the e-mail, is terribly offended when he is told of the complaint because he routinely receives similar information and believes it is well within his rights to use the sexual language and images because they are "everywhere on the net."

Relevant Questions

1. Is this free speech or could this be considered sexual harassment under Title IX?

Campus administrators and judicial officers may be legitimately confused when discerning the differences between harassment (sexual in this case) and free speech. It is strongly recommended that readers review *Revised Sexual Harassment Guidance: Harassment of Students by*

School Employees, Other Students or Third Parties (OCR, 2001) available at www.ed.gov/ocr/shguide/. According to this guide, sexual harassment of students can constitute discrimination prohibited by Title IX.

> Sexual harassment is unwelcome conduct of a sexual nature. Sexual harassment can include unwelcome sexual advances, requests for sexual favors and other verbal, non-verbal or physical conduct of a sexual nature. Sexual harassment of a student can deny or limit, on the basis of sex, the student's ability to participate in or receive benefits and services or opportunities in the school's program.

Two types of harassment are generally recognized: *Quid pro quo* (e.g., a university employee requests sexual favors from a student in exchange for a better grade) and hostile environment in which the alleged victim's environment is so "poisoned" by the conduct of another (student, staff, faculty, visitor to campus) that the student is unable to benefit from the academic or co-curricular program. Note that the term "school" used in the policy applies to elementary and secondary schools as well as colleges or universities.

> The school has notice of harassment if a responsible school employee actually knew or, in the exercise of reasonable care, should have known about the harassment.

> The school has a duty upon notice of the harassment to take prompt and effective action to stop the harassment and prevent recurrence. (OCR, 2001)

In this scenario, this behavior meets the threshold identified by

OCR (severe or pervasive), and it appears that the behavior is, indeed, sexual harassment. The behavior is unwelcome, of a sexual nature, and so severe and pervasive (by a reasonable person taking into account similar circumstances including the victim's age and gender) as to deny Allyson the benefits of the education program. The harassment has affected her education. She has reported the incidents to a university employee, someone whom she believes can take appropriate action. The university has an obligation to stop the harassment, prevent its reoccurrence, and rectify the effects of the harassment and prevent retaliation.

If the scenario noted only one or two incidents (instead of 22 incidents) of unwelcome e-mail that did not meet the OCR threshold, would the university have any obligation to take action? The authors believe that the answer would be "yes" if the student filed a complaint or discussed concerns with a staff member. "Action" does not necessarily imply a complaint that is formally adjudicated. A staff member from the lab could recommend or even help Allyson send a response to Brian asking that he stop sending her e-mail. If he fails to honor this request, additional steps, including a more formal complaint would be warranted. The lab assistant or other supervisor could also meet with Brian to discuss sexual harassment and even withdraw computer privileges if necessary. Sometimes face-to-face meetings with a supervisor can be developmental and stop the juvenile behavior before it reaches the level of sexual harassment. Careful documentation of action steps taken to resolve such matters will be of vital importance if further action is needed.

2. Is this protected speech or could this be considered obscenity?

Photos from generally available publications such as *Hustler* are probably not considered obscene, especially in a college environment. Obscenity is defined quite specifically by the Court in *Miller v. California* as confined "to works which depict or describe sexual conduct." The *Miller* Court stated that the work, taken as a whole, must appeal to the prurient interest in sex; portray sexual conduct in a patently offensive way; and, when taken as a whole not have serious literary, artistic, political, or scientific value (*First Amendment Annotations*, 2006). While the material may be offensive, that is a matter of personal taste, and administrators may be better off addressing this incident under other standards, such as a copyright violation.

Images of child pornography are always illegal under federal law.

3. Can your campus technology office address copyright issues such as the use of the pictures from *Hustler*?

Yes. It is illegal to use (copy and use) copyrighted information from this and similar magazines. Sometimes dealing with the copyright issue is less problematic than addressing whether any given material is obscene or not. Chronic misuse of this or similar policies may result in suspending the use of university computing resources.

4. Once a staff member is made aware of the alleged harassment, does he/she have a duty to act?

Yes. *Davis v. Monroe County Board of Education* established the concept of "deliberate indifference." Deliberate indifference means that someone empowered to act knew and chose not to act or did not act appropriately to redress the harassment. The lab monitor should be trained in such matters and therefore empowered to act even if the "act" is to notify his or her superior of the concern.

The Court in the above case stated that where it can be shown that the school has been deliberately indifferent, the liability standards established in those cases are limited to private action for monetary damages (OCR, 2001).

Additional Tips

★ It is imperative to have clear policies for the prevention of sexual harassment as well as employee training, especially for employees who supervise others. Readers should consult the *Revised Sexual Harassment Guidance: Harassment of Students by School Employees, Other Students or Third Parties* (2001). This document outlines steps that must be taken to prevent sexual harassment on campus. The Web address is http://www.ed.gov/print/about/offices/list/ocr/docs/shguide.html.

★ Campuses are required to create and widely publicize their policies regarding sexual harassment of students and employees.

★ Additionally, campuses must identify and publicize the name and phone number of the Title IX officer who is charged with receiving and investigating allegations of sexual harassment/assault under Title IX. Sometimes this role is assumed by the campus judicial officer, the affirmative action officer, or both. They must consider whether the behavior is sufficiently severe or pervasive to require action. Such action does not necessarily imply suspension or expulsion. It must be (as with all cases) appropriate to redress the harm and prevent recurrence.

★ Administrators may wish to provide training to staff on the broad reach of Title IX (beyond athletics).

SCENARIO 3. CAMPUS PREACHER

"Preacher Bob" is requesting a permit to preach the gospel on Mondays, Wednesdays, and Fridays from noon to 5 p.m. in the most public area of campus. Bob is well-versed in his rights regarding free speech. Surrounded by a sizeable crowd of bored students, he blows his police whistle at women passing by and states loudly, "Women with short hair and women who wear slacks are whores and are doomed to burn in hell. They will be kept company by the fornicators, druggies, and, of course, the homosexuals and Catholics." Preacher Bob does this in the name of the Lord as a public service.

Relevant Questions

1. Is this free speech or harassment? What "test" should be used to determine this?

If the issue is a question of harassment, the reader would be advised to read the language contained in Title IX as well as the previously mentioned OCR Guidelines. When the issue is one of harassment based on race, national origin, etc., language in Title VI addresses such issues in a parallel manner. In either case, to lose First Amendment protection, the expression would need to be so severe or pervasive as to deny an individual the ability to benefit from educational programs and services. This is a high standard to meet and it would be difficult to argue that Bob's speech, no matter how offensive, meets that standard. Individuals are free to come and go from the area where Bob is speaking. They are not considered a captive audience.

Although such expression may not meet the strict definition of racial or sexual harassment, many may still consider it to be offensive. As Barron and Dienes wrote, however:

> In short, at this time, offensive speech is fully protected speech. While there are categories of unprotected expression, the Supreme Court has been quite insistent that offensive speech is not one of them.
>
> Whether the various contemporary movements to enact specific laws directed at hate speech or female pornography or indecency will create exceptions to this principle remains to be seen. (Barron & Dienes, 2004, p. 204)

2. Is the campus mall automatically considered a public forum?

Not necessarily, though a campus mall is probably a public forum (by its history or tradition) or a designated public forum, depending on its typical use and the institution's designation of the space. This question addresses one of the most fundamental concepts related to First Amendment issues on a college campus. Because of that, the answer to this question is purposely long. Gary Pavela, author of the *ASJA Law and Policy Report,* provided an excellent analysis of types of forums critical to understanding the nature of First Amendment issues.

[1] The fact that property is owned by the government does *not* mean that everyone has unlimited access to it.

[2] Deciding the scope of First Amendment protection on government-owned property requires courts to determine whether

the property is a traditional public forum, a designated public forum (further delineated being "limited" or "unlimited"), or a nonpublic forum.

[3] In traditional public forums ("places which by long tradition or by government fiat have been devoted to assembly and debate"), expression will be entitled to the highest First Amendment protection. Content-based restriction in these settings "must be necessary to serve a compelling government interest and be narrowly drawn to achieve that interest."

[4] "In unlimited designated public forums, the government may enforce a content-neutral time, place, and manner restriction only if the restriction is necessary to serve a significant government interest and is narrowly drawn to achieve that interest..."

[5] "In limited designated public forums, '[r]estrictions on speech not within the type of expression allowed in a limited public forum must only be reasonable and viewpoint neutral.'"

[6] "In a nonpublic forum, the government may restrict [all] speech 'as long as the restrictions are reasonable and [are] not an effort to suppress expression merely because the public officials oppose [a] speaker's view."

[7] College campuses consist of several different kinds of "forums." Otherwise, lawful expression in front of the student union (e.g., an unlimited designated public forum) may be barred in a concert hall (a limited designated public forum).

[8] In what may be the most controversial part of its ruling, a majority of the three-judge court in *Bowman* held that central locations on campus (like malls or sidewalks) should be considered "unlimited designated public forums," not "traditional public forums." A third judge (who agreed with the case outcome)

disagreed with that perspective, and observed that "I cannot adopt the Court's view as to public areas on a public university campus not being traditional public fora but instead designated public fora which the University can redesignate to a non-public forum on a whim." (Pavela, 2006, p. 1-2)

A recent formulation is that a time, place, or manner regulation "must be narrowly tailored to serve the government's legitimate content-neutral interests, but...need not be the least-restrictive or least-intrusive means of doing so" (*First Amendment Annotations*, 2006).

3. Is Preacher Bob's rhetoric (perceived as hateful to some individuals and groups) considered fighting words?

No. Some observers will claim that Preacher Bob's rhetoric is considered "fighting words" (*Chaplinsky v. New Hampshire*) or "hate speech" and wonder why Preacher Bob is allowed to speak on campus at all. "Fighting words" is an old term embedded in case law. It applies to "toe to toe" confrontations in which the words "said to the person of the hearer" tend to provoke an immediate breach of peace. Campus preachers are typically keenly aware of First Amendment law and are careful not to engage individuals in this manner. Although "hate speech" is a commonly used term, it has no legal definition and is not, in and of itself, a category of prohibited speech.

4. Can an institution legally limit the number of times any one person (not affiliated with campus) may speak during any one semester?

Although an institution could probably start with a limit, a speaker may not be denied further space that no one else is using. This specific question was recently answered by the U.S. Court of Appeals for the 8th Circuit in *Bowman v. White* 444 F.3d 967, 2006.

The case involved a campus preacher named Gary Bowman who believed his First Amendment rights had been violated when a public university in Arkansas attempted to limit the number of times he could speak on campus in a single year. Other limitations were also applied which the Court upheld. A summary of select finding appears below.

> The appeals court's ruling on the five-visit rule noted that the university put forth a "significant" argument on behalf of its policy: that it "fosters a diversity of usage" and "prevents the monopolization of space." While those are valuable goals, the court found that the rule was not "sufficiently narrow," given the strong presumption in favor of free speech. The ruling noted that there are days for which there are no requests to use various campus spaces. As a result, the court found, the policy can have the impact of limiting Bowman's speech without advancing any worthy goal.

> The university could, the court ruled, have a policy that starts off with a limit of five, and that would prevent any group from signing up for too many days, as long as there were also procedures to open up unused space later to interested parties. The university could even favor for such space groups that haven't previously signed up, the court said. The only ban was on an absolute limit, regardless of whether anyone else wanted the space. (Jaschik, 2006)

5. Can a campus require a speaker to obtain a permit before speaking on campus?

This question was also answered (for Circuit 8) in the *Bowman* decision. A different conclusion could be reached by another court in a different circuit.

> The other rules challenged by Bowman were clearly constitutional, the court found. Requiring a permit, and requiring a permit three days in advance, the court found, were legitimate ways for the university to deal with its "significant public safety interest." (As it relates to Bowman, this need is not just theoretical: Security officers have had to set up barriers to deal with unruly, angry crowds during his visits.) As for the limits on appearances during "dead days" on which students prepare for and take final exams, the court found that this ban was reasonable and related to the university's "educational mission." (Jaschik, 2006)

FIRE and other First Amendment watch-dog groups will argue that permits are problematic, if necessary, and may lead to administrative abuse. For example, administrative bias or abuse might occur if the secretary or a student worker who collects the permits and makes assignments to various available areas of campus gives the best spots to those that they agree with most. Assignments should not be based on the perceived value of the speaker's message but on content-neutral criteria such as the date the reservation was made.

6. If the preacher is disruptive to the classes being held nearby, can he be moved?

Yes. Teaching is a legitimate function of the university and maintaining an environment conducive to that function is of vital importance (a compelling governmental interest). If the speaker disturbs that environment, he or she may be legitimately moved. The alternative location selected must be comparable, and provide ample alternative means of communicating the message (e.g., the speaker may not be moved to an out-of-the-way location with a significantly lower volume of traffic). The university may not move the speaker because it finds his message offensive.

In addition, Preacher Bob may be prevented from using amplification so classes won't be disturbed (a content-neutral time, place, and manner restriction that is narrowly tailored), but that manner of restriction must be applied equally to other speakers. Many students and even some faculty and staff are extremely offended by Bob's remarks and complain bitterly to the administration and even file complaints with the judicial officer. They may have heard that the university has "zero tolerance" for discrimination so why does it permit this man on campus? The court in *Papish* wrote, "The mere dissemination of ideas—no matter how offensive to good taste—on a state university campus may not be shut off in the name alone of conventions of decency." While the *Papish* case dealt with freedom of the press, it applies to all First Amendment issues. It is important to help students understand that they are not "captive." They are free to leave the area where Preacher Bob is speaking or avoid it altogether. The university may legitimately prohibit Bob from "preaching" in a cafeteria or classroom, where his speaking may be disruptive to the intended purpose of the space.

7. If the campus has evidence that complaints follow Bob's visits, can he be moved to an isolated location on campus?

No. Dislike for Preacher Bob's message may not dictate his placement on campus to, for example, tiny speech zones located away from the core of campus.

8. May the preacher be removed if the audience grows upset or even angry?

No. The speech being expressed does not constitute harassment, "fighting words," or a specific threat, even though it may stir strong emotion in the listeners. As Supreme Court Justice Oliver Wendell Holmes so appropriately reminded us in the *Cohen* case, the purpose of the First Amendment is to protect all thought (speech); not just those thoughts that we agree with but also that which we hate.

Additional Tips

★   The campus may want to designate monitors to observe the behavior of the crowd and protect Preacher Bob from those that get excited by his rhetoric. Monitors must be properly trained to observe and respond to behavior that threatens the speaker. Having monitors working in the crowd affords a great opportunity to educate students about the First Amendment.

★   If the behavior of students or others in the audience violates any law or portion of the conduct code, police and/or the campus judicial officer should take appropriate action.

★   If permits are utilized, all staff and student workers who issue them should be appropriately trained and understand that such permits must be issued on a content-neutral basis.

★ If a person is speaking without having secured a campus-re-
quired permit, yet is in an area that is designated as a limited
public forum and is not disturbing or conflicting with permitted activities, it may be wise to let that person be.

SCENARIO 4. GAY STUDENT ALLIANCE—GROUP RECOGNITION

At a conservative public university, the Gay and Lesbian
Student Association (GLSA) requests that its group be formally
recognized by the Student Government Association so that it can
be eligible for student fee funds. Several conservative student
groups, their advisors, and campus administrators have spoken
against the recognition because GLSA's values are inconsistent
with the enacted values of the university, and they fear that the
group will promote sodomy and other illegal acts prohibited by
state law.

Relevant Questions

**1. Can this group be blocked from recognition because the
group's espoused beliefs conflict with those of members of the
student body, the university, administration, and the Board of
Regents?**

No. A group may not be excluded from a public university based
on its beliefs. Quoting Justice John M. Harlan:

> Effective advocacy of both public and private points
> of view, particularly controversial ones, is undeniably
> enhanced by group association, as this court has more
> than once recognized by remarking on the close nexus

between the freedoms of speech and assembly...It is beyond debate that freedom to engage in association for the advancement of beliefs and ideas is an inseparable aspect of the "liberty" as assured by the Due Process Clause of the Fourteenth Amendment which embraces freedom of speech. (Fuson, 1995, p. 326)

Cases similar to the incident described in the scenario have been heard by the courts (*Gay Student Services v. Texas A&M University*, *Gay Alliance of Students v. Matthews,* and *Gay Lib v. University of Missouri*). In all of those cases, the courts have primarily relied on the findings in *Healy v. James* and *Tinker v. DesMoines. Healy* specifically dealt with students who wanted to develop and have recognized a chapter of the Students for a Democratic Society (SDS) on campus. The administrators, concerned that national SDS chapters had been linked to campus disturbances elsewhere, wanted to block the chapter's recognition. The administrators' logic did not move the courts. In *Tinker*, the Court ruled that undifferentiated fear or apprehension of disturbance (in this case, by high school students wearing black armbands in protest of the Vietnam War) was not enough to overcome the right of freedom of expression.

The *Healy* Court stated, "There can be no doubt that denial of official recognition without justification to college organizations burdens or abridges the First Amendment freedom of association."

In the cases mentioned above, the campus administrators believed that recognizing the group in question would create political issues or problems, and they believed this rationale was a compelling state interest. The courts found these arguments insufficient to justify a governmental prior restraint on the right of the groups to associate for the purposes avowed in their mission/purpose statements.

The Court in *Gay Student Services v. Texas A&M University* said, "We think that on this record TAMU's [Texas A&M University's] public health argument (homosexual students are more prone to depression than heterosexuals) is precisely the 'undifferentiated fear or apprehension' that the Supreme Court has repeatedly held 'is not enough to overcome the right to freedom of expression'" (*Tinker* and *Healy*).

In *Gay Lib*, the Eighth Circuit concluded that denying recognition to a gay group "smacks of penalizing persons for their status rather than their conduct which is constitutionally impermissible" (*Robinson v. California*).

In *Rosenberger* (1995), the Courts made it clear that to preserve viewpoint neutrality in making their decisions about funding, public universities may not take into account or consider what position or opinion a student or group of students stand(s) for or advocate(s).

2. Can a university deny funding (from student fees or other sources) for a recognized student group if some students complain that they disagree with the group's stated purpose?

No. As the Supreme Court held in *University of Wisconsin v. Southworth*, decisions regarding the funding of student organizations must be made in a content-neutral manner. The same logic would apply to any group some students were opposed to funding, whether a White supremacist group, the college Republicans, or a gay/lesbian/bisexual group.

3. Can a private college deny recognition or funding to a student group whose mission conflicts with the institutions' values?

Yes, it can. The First Amendment refers to "governmental action."

Private institutions are not "state actors" and would be free to establish policies for recognition or funding consistent with their stated purpose or values.

Additional Tip

★   As funding decisions are often made by committees of students, it would be prudent to provide training so that these students understand the concept and mandate of content neutrality.

Scenario 5. Campus Newspaper—The Holocaust

The university paper is asked to insert a long advertisement regarding the Holocaust and World War II history in its next edition. The (student) assistant editor for advertising briefly reviews the copy and sends it to the printer. The insert is actually a revisionist's account of World War II stating that the Holocaust was a hoax. When the paper hits the campus the next day, calls start coming into the president's office, the student newspaper office, and the judicial affairs office demanding to know why the university allowed such clearly anti-Semitic rhetoric to be distributed. The callers demand that the university expel the student editor, fire the faculty advisor, and immediately apologize to the Jewish faculty, staff, and students.

Relevant Questions

1. Did running the advertisement in the student paper create a hostile environment as several faculty, staff, and students contend?

No. Although the advertisement may certainly have created a tense or uncomfortable environment, this singular incident would not meet the threshold for creating a hostile environment. Hostile environment theory has been discussed extensively in earlier scenarios. While campus members may be shocked and offended by what they read, the perceived harassment is not so severe or pervasive as to deny a reasonable person the benefits of the educational program.

2. Is this indeed a form of "hate" speech?

Although this advertisement may be considered hateful, there is no prohibition against "hate" speech. While this term has appeared quite often in the literature, it is not a category of prohibited speech in and of itself. This term is often confused with the seldom used "fighting words" doctrine; however, this advertisement does not fit the criteria of "fighting words" (see *Chaplinsky*).

3. Had the university been aware of the insert before it was published, could the university have blocked its release?

Probably not. Prior to *Hosty v. Carter*, the answer would have been a more resounding "no;" however, based on this Circuit 7 decision it appears that this issue is shifting a bit. As discussed in *Inside Higher Ed* (Feb. 22, 2006), the decision has two new twists: whether the paper is a designated public forum and whether the newspaper's funding source affects editorial control. It will be interesting to see how *Hosty* will impact subsequent decisions.

Even though administrators may disagree with the decisions of the student press, there is no question that a free press is critical to a democratic society. Thomas Jefferson believed so strongly in freedom of the press that he once said: "If it were left to me to decide whether we should have a government without a free press or a free press without a government, I would prefer the latter" (Monk, 1991, p. 73).

4. Can the university indeed take disciplinary action against the student or faculty member responsible?

If there is no violation of the campus code, there should be no finding or sanction involved. In this scenario, the campus newspaper printed (perhaps accidentally) a long advertisement that was patently offensive to many on campus. It did not necessarily create a hostile environment in the legal sense. It also did not reflect "fighting words," in that it was unlikely to create an immediate breach of peace and was not directed to an individual or "the person of the hearer." Depending on the campus newspaper's policies, the newspaper staff might have omitted this material from the newspaper if they had reviewed it more carefully. The campus administration would be wise to address the incident through a public forum or debate on the issue but avoid taking disciplinary action against the faculty advisor or student editor.

The court in *Papish* reflecting on *Healy* said, "We think *Healy* makes it clear that the mere dissemination of ideas—no matter how offensive to good taste on a state university campus may not be shut off in the name alone of "conventions of decency."

In *Papish*, a decision to expel a student editor for reprinting a controversial, offensive cartoon and using a headline perceived to be obscene by the administration was overturned using the reasoning in *Healy*.

Dissenting in *Papish*, Justice Warren E. Burger said the following:

> Students are, of course, free to criticize the university, its faculty or the government in vigorous or even harsh

terms. But it is not unreasonable or violative of the Constitution to subject to disciplinary action those individuals who distribute publications which are at the same time obscene and infantile. To preclude a state university or college from regulating the distribution of such obscene malice does not protect the values inherent in the First Amendment; rather, it demeans those values.

In the final analysis, the court weighed in on the side of the First Amendment.

Additional Tips

★ Campuses facing similar upheaval should fight speech with speech. While the paper's staff may or may not feel compelled to apologize for its insensitivity or mistake, the administration can use this opportunity to discuss both the Holocaust and the First Amendment in a variety of different settings.

★ Ensure that all campus newspaper advisors have an understanding of relevant First Amendment issues.

SCENARIO 6. ABC FRATERNITY COSTUME PARTY—SYMBOLIC SPEECH

A university-recognized fraternity hosts a costume party off-campus with invited guests and dates. One member, dressed as a Ku Klux Klansman, pretends to hang a man in blackface wearing a prisoner's uniform. A third man is pictured holding a bullwhip above the head of the "prisoner." These behaviors, immortalized on film, are available for purchase on the hired photographer's

100

Web site protected by the super-secret password, "Greek." The site is reported to Tolerance.org, a branch of the Southern Poverty Law Center. Several students become aware of these pictures and demand that the fraternity be suspended.

Relevant Questions

1. Can and/or should the university take disciplinary action(s) against the fraternity?

No action should be taken based on the symbolic speech; however, if other policies were violated (alcohol, noise, etc.), the university could take disciplinary action if there was adequate evidence or an admission of the violation.

A useful legal reference for this scenario is *Iota Xi Chapter of Sigma Chi Fraternity v. George Mason University*. What these two incidents share is campus upheaval caused by the incivility, insensitivity, and perhaps even racism of fellow students. In the *Iota Xi* case, or "Ugly Woman" case as it is commonly referred to, men dressed in women's clothing with one in blackface displaying exaggerated stereotyped features. George Mason University imposed disciplinary sanctions against the fraternity. Iota appealed and won. George Mason appealed that decision and lost. George Mason University indicated to the Court that failing to impose sanctions against the fraternity would hurt its ability to recruit and retain minority students at George Mason. Notably, George Mason, the university's namesake, was a slave owner. George Mason University had worked very hard to increase underrepresented student enrollment and this, it believed, was a compelling governmental interest that justified the actions it took.

One key difference between the scenarios is that the Ugly

Woman performance was an entertainment venue with tickets sold and the ABC Fraternity incident was a private costume party off campus.

> The Court found that that the First Amendment protects non-obscene live entertainment because of its expressive character. Although admittedly offensive and of very low quality, the contest was in the form of a skit and constituted inherently expressive entertainment; as such, the Court ruled, it was entitled to full First Amendment protection. (*Iota Xi Chapter of Sigma Chi Fraternity v. George Mason University*)

2. Can the national fraternity office or the Interfraternity Council (IFC) of the college or university take action(s) even if the university does not?

Yes. National offices should be asked to become involved. The Interfraternity Council on campus may also have policies that may have been violated (alcohol, as underage drinking was observed in the photos) and that may be actionable by them. Their actions would be based on their policies and do not reflect state action.

3. If the university asks that IFC prevent such costumes or costume parties, could this be considered prior restraint of speech?

Nothing would prevent the IFC from developing policies of its own; however, if the university took the same step, it would likely be considered prior restraint of speech, in clear violation of the First Amendment.

Additional Tips

★ In situations where disciplinary action by the university is not warranted, action to discuss the behavior and address its impact is needed. Vigils and other university- or student-sponsored activities allow the university to address racist behavior (even if unintentional) and the First Amendment.

★ An ideal outcome would be to have the members of the chapter apply self-imposed "sanctions" to make amends to the campus community.

Scenario 7. Confederate Flag

Jake hangs a Confederate flag on the outside of his residence hall window. Residents complain to the hall director that the flag is a symbol of hate and must be immediately removed. Other posters and flags can be observed from the outside of the building.

Relevant Questions

1. Can/should the university prohibit just the Confederate flag or other similar images that may illicit hurt feelings, anger, and the possibility of retribution to the owner of the flag?

The most important consideration in this scenario is content neutrality. Even though the presence of the flag may cause emotional distress, courts have held that such distress, by itself, is not enough to regulate speech. Prohibiting only certain symbols (in this case, the

Confederate flag) is unconstitutional because it violates the doctrine of content neutrality.

2. Could an institution prohibit all door hangings?

The institution could prohibit all hangings if there is a compelling state interest for doing so, such as prohibiting the hanging of any material on the outside of room doors to avoid such materials being set on fire.

Additional Tip

★ These issues are fraught with emotionally charged viewpoints within and among groups. Even if the incident is not formally actionable, meeting with the residents involved to discuss their behavior and motivation is critical.

SCENARIO 8. PROFANITY AT SPORTING EVENTS

Pigskin U. is a Division I school with a first-rate football team whose games are often nationally televised. After last Saturday's game, an irate member of the Alumni Club calls the president claiming he had to leave the game with his two young children because the language and behavior of the students present was obscene and out of control. The president asks an administrator to work with campus police and stadium security staff to deal with these foul-mouthed fans.

Relevant Questions

1. Is foul language by students protected as free speech?

Most likely. Several articles discussing fan behavior have surfaced recently. The best and most comprehensive discussion is that of Howard M. Wasserman, who noted:

> Many free-speech controversies, especially on college campuses, are grounded in concerns for civility, politeness and good taste. They also tend to follow the same path and end the same way. A government entity regulates speech in an effort to elevate discourse, limit the profane and protect public and personal sensitivities; courts strike down the regulations as violating the First Amendment freedom of speech; and we end up right where we started. (Wasserman, 2004)

2. Does such language constitute obscenity?

No. Obscenity was defined by the U.S. Supreme Court, in *Miller v. California*, which established a three-part test. This test stated that the Constitution will not protect speech and expression that:

★ Taken as a whole, would be found by an average person to appeal to prurient interests, when "community standards" are applied

★ Depicts or describes, in a patently offensive way, sexual conduct specifically defined by state law

★ Taken as a whole, lacks serious literary, artistic, political, or scientific merit

One would be hard pressed to find even the most obnoxious fan behavior reaching this level. Wasserman put it quite eloquently when he wrote:

> It is difficult to reconcile that "Fuck the draft" is a protected message in a courthouse, but "Fuck Duke" is unprotected amid the cacophony of 20,000 screaming basketball fans. It is even less comprehensible that Paul Cohen's (See *Cohen*) intellectual heir could be prohibited from wearing his jacket (for example, to protest the so-called "backdoor draft" created by extending reservists' service) at a university sports arena governed by a fan speech code. (Wasserman, 2004)

3. Could attendees at a sporting event be considered a "captive audience"?

Although some may argue that attendees at a sporting event required to sit in assigned seats are captive, the reality is that no one is forcing individuals to attend the athletic event. As Wasserman explained:

> Courts have found listeners to be captives in only four places: their own homes, the workplace, public elementary and secondary schools, and inside and around abortion clinics. And even in those places, captive-audience status permits government to limit oral expression but not the same message in written form on pickets, signs or clothing. One certainly could avert one's eyes to avoid viewing the message written on a sign or on the body of a student at a basketball game.

Of course, one problem with cheering speech is that much of it is oral. Fans have complained not only about signs and T-shirts but also about chants and taunts targeting players, coaches, and officials, which other fans may be unable to avoid no matter where in the arena they sit. Objectors must perform the more difficult task of averting their ears to avoid offensive cheers, something that children may be even less able to do. It is true that courts have upheld content-neutral regulations on sound and noise levels to protect captive audiences, beginning with the Supreme Court case *Kovacs v. Cooper* in 1949. But government never has been permitted to protect captive auditors by singling out particular profane or offensive oral messages for selective restriction while leaving related messages on the same subject, uttered at the same volume, undisturbed.

More important, the captive-audience doctrine never has been applied to listeners in public places of recreation and entertainment, places to which people voluntarily go for the particular purpose of engaging in expressive activity, in this case cheering on their favorite college team. Fans who pay to attend a college basketball game at an on-campus arena are not captive auditors there, any more than an individual walking on a city street who stumbles across an objectionable political rally or an individual whose office sits above the route of an objectionable parade. (Wasserman, 2004)

Additional Tips

★ Several campuses have successfully used student peer monitors, (volunteer student leaders and athletes from different sports) to help address fans' aberrant behavior. With minimal basic training, these students agree to sit in the stands in problematic areas of the arena and apply gentle persuasion to illicit the desired behavioral change. Having them say, for example, "that is not cool" to a particularly offensive remark may be enough to stop or de-escalate the negative behavior.

★ If someone's behavior is so egregious at the game that it prevents others from viewing the game, the behavior (not speech) can be dealt with by stadium staff. An example might include someone flailing their arms so wildly that people seated next to them fear they will be struck.

Scenario 9. Fighting Words

Michael, an African American student, has never gotten along with Tyler, a Caucasian student who lives down the hall from him. Today, Michael comes to an administrator's office and complains that Tyler walked up to him in the hall last night and said, "Why don't you just go back to the ghetto, you f_ _ _ _ _ g n_ _ _ _ r." Michael was so angry that he immediately punched Tyler.

Relevant Questions

1. Can and/or should the university take disciplinary action(s) against Tyler for what he said?

The answer depends largely on personal interpretation of standards. Some may argue that Tyler's speech constituted "fighting words" and, as such, was not protected by the First Amendment.

In order to meet the standard of "fighting words," speech must be "toe to toe" (i.e., said directly to the other person), and must be of such a nature that it would provoke a reasonable person to an immediate breach of peace. It is incredibly difficult to evaluate exactly what speech would rise to this level for a "reasonable person," and one may argue that any competent adult should have the self-control to avoid such an immediate violent reaction.

In this scenario, Tyler's words were clearly explosive, were said "toe to toe," and resulted in an immediate breach of peace. Unless other mitigating factors come into play, this *might* be a case where the "fighting words" doctrine could apply. Again, it depends on how the standards are interpreted in contemporary society.

The "fighting words" doctrine is fairly old (1942) and societal expectations have changed considerably since that time, so it would be fairly difficult to meet such a standard. Pavela said, "At present, the fighting words doctrine is probably limited to provocative, face-to-face encounters that might also be treated as physical threats or intimidation." (Pavela, 2004, p. 3215)

2. Do Tyler's comments constitute harassment?

Probably not. According to Title VI guidelines, harassment must be so severe and pervasive as to deny an individual the benefits of an education program. If this behavior continued, it may certainly be deemed to rise to that level but a one-time incident probably would not.

Additional Tips

★ If a complaint is filed about Michael's behavior for assaulting Tyler, the adjudicator may consider the way in which Tyler provoked the action in the investigation and decision.

★ It is important to communicate the institution's values related to civility and diversity and to reinforce this in the halls and as many different venues as possible.

SCENARIO 10. GAY PRIDE POSTER ABLAZE

Aaron, Josh, and Sean set fire to a gay pride poster on Andrew's residence hall door. Andrew is openly gay. A witness tells staff members that she had seen the three men set the poster on fire. As a result, Aaron, Josh, and Sean admit having done so and further state that they did so because they "hated fags and hoped it would cause Andrew to move out."

Relevant Questions

1. Is the statement "hate fags" considered protected speech?

A simple statement that someone "hates fags" is, indeed, protected speech. Although the words may cause distress, disagreement, and anger, they do not constitute "fighting words," harassment, defamation, or any other category of unprotected speech.

2. Although it's obvious the men may be held accountable for setting the fire, can the institution increase the penalty because of their motivation?

If the men are found responsible for setting the fire, the penalty may be enhanced due to their own admission that the fire was set because of their bias. Colleges and universities wishing to consider penalty enhancement should discuss this possibility with their legal counsel. Before penalty enhancement could be considered in this case, a written policy would need to be contained within the residence hall agreement and/or code of conduct in advance of its use.

Wisconsin v. Mitchell examined the constitutionality of a state law that enhanced the criminal penalty for a crime when the victim was chosen because of "race, religion, color, disability, sexual orientation, national origin, or ancestry." It is important to note that this enhanced penalty was only upheld because the victim of the crime was specifically selected due to bias. In this scenario, the men's admission that they specifically set the fire **because they "hated fags"** provides a direct correlation between their beliefs and the selection of the victim. If the men had set the fire and had not made that statement, even if they were known to hold such beliefs, it would not meet the test for a bias-motivated penalty enhancement.

Educators always have the opportunity to discuss behavior (dangerous or disruptive) that affects students. The men in the scenario are free to have and express homophobic attitudes and beliefs but may not threaten or intimidate a resident who is gay.

Additional Tips

★ Penalty enhancement is controversial and should be considered only after a robust campus discussion.

★ On campuses where penalty enhancement has been used successfully, it requires two steps—a finding of responsibility on the particular code of conduct violation and then a separate decision to determine if the behavior was motivated by bias. Typically, the penalty would be increased one "level." For example, an offense that would receive a letter of reprimand would be increased to probation.

SCENARIO 11. BLOG ME!

Erin and Alex were high school sweethearts who broke up late in the summer before starting college. Subsequently, Erin slept with one of Alex's friends, and Alex began posting blogs about Erin with statements such as: "You are a whore and like to sleep in bed with pretty frat guys. If you want to f--k, call her at ********." In several e-mails, Alex also says that he would "get her" for treating him so poorly.

Erin's parents contact the administration, demanding that someone make Alex stop the postings and take serious disciplinary action against Alex for sexual harassment. They are also concerned about her safety because of his reference to "getting her." They believe this to be a direct threat to her safety.

Relevant Questions

1. Can the university require Alex to stop posting such blogs?

No, unless his comments fall into a category of unprotected speech or conflict with university computing policies. Such Web sites would be considered public forums and their intended purpose is the posting of expression.

2. Is this sexual harassment?

No. The "Dear Colleague" letter from the Office for Civil Rights contains the following guidance:

> Some colleges and universities have interpreted OCR's prohibition of 'harassment' as encompassing all offensive speech regarding sex, disability, race or other classifications. Harassment, however, to be prohibited by the statutes within OCR's jurisdiction, must include something beyond the mere expression of views, words, symbols or thoughts that some person finds offensive. Under OCR's standard, the conduct must also be considered sufficiently serious to deny or limit a student's ability to participate in or benefit from the educational program. Thus, OCR's standards require that the conduct be evaluated from the perspective of a reasonable person in the alleged victim's position, considering all the circumstances, including the alleged victim's age. (July 28, 2003)

Thus, in this scenario, Alex's conduct must be evaluated from the perspective of a reasonable person in Erin's position and must consider all of the circumstances. Typically, these are tit-for-tat blogs. The fact that the postings are on a Web site and Erin does not have to be exposed to them may be a salient factor.

Although this may not rise to the level of sexual harassment, the material may still be considered offensive, however, as Barron and Dienes noted:

> In short, at this time, offensive speech is fully protected speech. While there are categories of unprotected ex-

pression, the Supreme Court has been quite insistent that offensive speech is not one of them.

Whether the various contemporary movements to enact specific laws directed at hate speech or female pornography or indecency will create exceptions to this principle remains to be seen. (Barron & Dienes, 2004, p. 92-93)

3. Should the university address defamation?

The definition of defamation remains the same, even if the medium is electronic, rather than verbal or traditional print. It could be addressed but not necessarily in a disciplinary setting. To attempt to hold someone accountable for defamation, the university would first need to determine if the information posted is indeed false and if someone's reputation was indeed harmed. Defamation cases are generally reserved for civil courts and not the campus.

4. Does Alex's statement about "getting her" reflect an actionable threat?

Probably not. Although the sense of threat is usually in the eyes of the beholder, a reasonable person might not consider this to be a specific threat worthy of action. A brief article on this topic at the First Amendment Center Web site, "How Do Courts Determine Whether Speech is a True Threat," said:

The Supreme Court has ruled that true threats receive no First Amendment protection. Unfortunately, the Court has not clearly defined a test for determining what types of speech constitute a true threat. As a result, the lower courts have adopted a variety of tests to determine whether speech constitutes a true threat.

Some courts have determined that "if a reasonable person would foresee that an objective rational recipient of the statement would interpret its language to constitute a serious expression...[then] the message conveys a 'true threat.'"

Other courts consider a series of factors in determining whether speech constitutes a true threat, including (1) the reaction of the recipient of the speech; (2) whether the threat was conditional; (3) whether the speaker communicated the speech directly to the recipient; (4) whether the speaker had made similar statements in the past; and (5) whether the recipient had reason to believe the speaker could engage in violence. (First Amendment Center, 2004)

Many cases regarding true threats made by students are just now circulating through the state and federal courts. Consequently, school officials are advised to seek legal counsel in this evolving area of the law.

Additional Tips

★ Facebook, Xanga, MySpace, and other blogs represent a new challenge for safety, claims of harassment, and other abuse. While access may be provided by the university, these sites are **not** monitored by the university. Comments are made and then refuted from all sides. University resources may be better spent encouraging students not to participate on these Web sites or, better still, to understand the inherent dangers of public discussions of private matters. Many blog sites have a complaint function on the screen. The university may not have to serve as the arbiter of the complaint, but rather encourage the aggrieved student to work directly with the blog site.

★ Blog site users can control access to their own pages and should be encouraged to do so.

★ The institution may wish to create educational brochures or Web sites regarding the potential consequences of participating in such blogs.

SCENARIO 12. DISRUPTIVE OUTBURSTS IN CLASS

Dr. Howard, a history professor, complains to the conduct officer that Rick, a student with whom he has a philosophical disagreement, consistently disrupts his class by long-winded argumentative outbursts that affect his ability to teach the class. Dr. Howard further states that other students have complained to him about this behavior.

Relevant Questions

1. Is this student's speech/behavior protected under the First Amendment?

Although Rick's ideas and thoughts would be constitutionally protected, his disruptive behavior would not be. Though we often think of *Tinker* as protecting a student's speech, the Court did note that behavior that materially disrupts class work or involves substantial disorder or invasion of the rights of others is, of course, not immunized by the constitutional guarantee of freedom of speech. In this scenario, Rick's viewpoint is not the issue. The issue is the manner in which he voices his opinions, which is deemed materially disruptive to the class and affects the teacher's ability to teach and the students' ability to learn. Content may be an issue if this is a history class and Rick wants to spend class time talking about cafeteria food. Viewpoint on a pertinent issue, however, may not be suppressed.

Many campuses include a prohibition against class disruption as part of the college or university code of conduct. Language from Texas A&M is provided as a sample and reads:

> 24.3.12 **Disruptive activity.** Participation in disruptive activity that interferes with teaching, research, administration, disciplinary proceedings, other University missions, processes, or functions including public-service functions, or other university activities. Such activities may include but are not limited to:
>
> ★ Leading or inciting others to disrupt scheduled and/or normal activities on university premises.
>
> ★ Classroom behavior that seriously interferes with either (a) the instructor's ability to conduct the class or (b) the ability of other students to profit from the instructional program.
>
> ★ Any behavior in class or out of class, which for any reason materially disrupts the classwork of others, involves substantial disorder, invades the rights of others, or otherwise disrupts the regular and essential operation of the University.

★ Activity or conduct that violates the Texas A&M University Rules on Freedom of Expression. (TAMU Student Code of Conduct, 2006)

2. If a student has a disability, can he or she be held accountable for disruptive behavior in the classroom as described in this scenario?

Yes. Disruptive behavior in the classroom is not acceptable. The focus by administrators and faculty involved needs to be on the disruption rather than the cause of the disruption.

Additional Tips

★ Faculty members are often at a loss as to how to regain control of a classroom situation such as this, which seems to be particularly common with new faculty. Academic advisors and judicial officers may wish to contact the student and point out why his style of communication is disruptive and recommend specific changes. Examples include raising one's hand to be recognized, minimizing emotionality, and being brief. Behavior modification has been found to work.

★ Faculty mentoring to improve assertiveness may also help.

★ Most disability services offices can provide advice on effectively dealing with specific disabilities. Such offices will often be willing to conduct training for faculty and staff.

SCENARIO 13. WHEN RELIGION COMES TO CAMPUS

The president's office routes an anonymous complaint from several students to the office of the vice president for student affairs. The students claim that their resident assistant (RA) is requiring students to attend Bible study on the floor to redress violations of hall policy such as noise, or visitation violations. The complaining students allege that the RA made a list of people who violated established hall rules and sent them a letter inviting them to attend a Bible study session in his room. If an invited student did not attend, he or she was threatened with more severe sanctions. The residents inform the university that "Bible study" is not contained as a sanction in the Residential Life Handbook. The students do not wish to be named but want this practice to stop immediately."

Relevant Questions

1. Can an institution prohibit an RA from conducting Bible studies or from participating in other forms of religious expression?

Probably not. There was a recent incident at a University of Wisconsin System institution involving this issue. The RA was told that he was not permitted to host any religious activities in his room. As a result of the RA filing a complaint, the UW system reconsidered its position in March of 2006 and developed the following policy:

> Resident Assistants are expected to work with student residents to create an open, inclusive, and supportive residential community. At the same time, because RA's are students themselves, they are encouraged to partici-

pate in campus activities and organizations. As such, RA's may participate in, organize, and lead any meetings or other activities, within their rooms, floors or residence halls, or anywhere else on campus, to the same extent as other students. However, they may not use their positions to inappropriately influence, pressure, or coerce student residents to attend or participate. (University of Wisconsin System press release, 2006)

Later chapters will discuss more fully how an individual or university decision can morph into a tsunami wave of controversy, public and private commentary (probably on both sides of the issue), and even a visit from FIRE. Excerpts from a FIRE press release dated March 14, 2006, illustrate this point. Readers may also wish to visit FIRE's Web site to view letters from Wisconsin legislators and other materials that give a sense of the intense interest and pressure surrounding First Amendment issues.

Case Highlights Lack of Respect for Freedom of Religion on Campuses Nationwide

MADISON, Wis., March 14, 2006—On Friday afternoon, the University of Wisconsin's (UW's) Board of Regents voted to protect religious liberty and freedom of expression on every UW campus. After six months of public pressure from the Foundation for Individual Rights in Education (FIRE), the Regents finally approved a policy that allows resident assistants (RAs) to lead Bible studies or any other meetings in their own dorm rooms.

"UW's decision to uphold religious liberty and freedom of expression is of national significance," stated FIRE Interim President Greg Lukianoff. "The 'Bible study ban' was unfair, unconstitutional, and highly unpopular."

The Bible study controversy began at the University of Wisconsin–Eau Claire (UWEC), where on July 26, 2005, a university administrator sent Christian RAs a letter ordering them to stop leading Bible studies in their dormitories. Administrators banned all voluntary studies of the Bible, Koran, and Torah that took place in the RAs' own rooms or anywhere in their own dormitories. The officials believed that holding such studies would make RAs less "approachable" to students who did not share their religion. FIRE subsequently discovered that UW–Madison, the system's flagship campus, enforced a similar ban.

In October 2005, FIRE launched a campaign to abolish the unjust "Bible study ban." FIRE asked UWEC Interim Chancellor Vicki Lord Larson to lift the ban on October 10 and took UWEC's repression public on November 2. This led to outcry from *USA Today*, newspapers across the Midwest, Fox News Channel, countless radio programs, and several Wisconsin legislators. Under pressure, UWEC suspended its ban on November 30 pending a system-wide review.

FIRE weighed in on that review process by writing to UW System President Kevin P. Reilly and to Wisconsin Attorney General Peggy A. Lautenschlager in defense of expressive rights on campus. FIRE also connected Lance

Steiger, the RA who bravely protested the ban, with attorneys from the Alliance Defense Fund (ADF), who
filed a lawsuit on his behalf.

After six months of constant coverage, the Board of Regents put an end to the controversy on Friday when it
approved a policy that gave RAs the right to "participate
in, organize, and lead any meetings or other activities,
within their rooms, floors or residence halls, or anywhere
else on campus, to the same extent as other students."

**2. Can Bible studies (or other forms of religious activities) be
required as part of the student disciplinary process?**

No, at least not at a public university. RAs should not be adjudi-
cating the case or applying sanctions. Typically the responsibility of an
RA is limited to documenting the alleged violation and forwarding it
up the "chain of command" where it can be heard and resolved. Some
clarification of the Constitutional principles of freedom of religion may
be helpful at this juncture.

According to Linda Monk, writing in *The Bill of Rights: A User's
Guide*:

As protected by the First Amendment, freedom of religion consists of two parts: the Establishment Clause and
the Free Exercise Clause. The Establishment Clause forbids the government from creating—or establishing—an
official church, formally supporting religious activities,
or giving preference to religion. But under the Free Exercise Clause, the government also can not interfere with

the expression of religious beliefs; sometimes these two rights conflict. (p. 42-42)

In *Lemon v. Kurtzman*, 1971, the Supreme Court set forth a three-part test, based on its holdings in previous cases, for determining whether a government policy violates the Establishment Clause: 1. The policy's purpose must be secular, not religious; 2. The policy's primary effect must neither advance nor inhibit religion; 3. The policy must avoid an "excessive entanglement" of government and religion. (p. 47)

Belief vs. Action. Freedom of religious belief is one of the very few absolute rights in the Bill of Rights. But religious beliefs often involve action, which government can regulate. (p. 55)

The very first Supreme Court case involving the Free Exercise Clause, *Reynolds v. United States 1879*, distinguished between belief and action. Reynolds was a Mormon living in Utah who had more than one wife, a practice known as polygamy. The Mormon Church advocated polygamy for its members but federal law prohibited it. The Supreme Court upheld Reynolds' conviction under federal law despite his religious beliefs... The Court noted, for example, that religious beliefs in human sacrifice would not exempt an individual from being prosecuted for murder. (Monk, 1991, p. 55-56)

Requiring Bible studies would appear to represent a clear violation of the Establishment Clause of the First Amendment, the origin of the concept of **separation of church and state.**

In addition to protecting religious freedom, the First Amendment protects a person's right to **not** declare a belief through action or words. Justice Robert H. Jackson, who wrote the opinion of the Court in *West Virginia State Board of Education v. Barnette* (1943), opined "[I]f there is any fixed star in our constitutional constellation, it is that no official, high or petty, can prescribe what shall be orthodox in politics, nationalism, religion or other matters of opinion or force citizens to confess by word or act their faith therein."

Additional Tips

★ Administrators should examine campus policies related to student employment that might restrict the First Amendment rights of students.

★ Administrators may wish to clarify employment expectations or boundaries (work hours, living arrangement such as in the residence hall, etc.) that may invite confusion or controversy.

★ Institutional judicial process and sanctioning guidelines should be evaluated to ensure clarity of ascribed roles and the authority to act, and train all staff accordingly.

BIBLIOGRAPHY

Barron, J. & Dienes, C.T. (2004). *First Amendment Law in a Nutshell* (3rd ed.). St. Paul, MN: West Publishing Company.

Constitutional Convention Members. (1787). The Constitution of the United States of America [Electronic Version]. Retrieved July 6, 2006 from http://www.archives.gov/national-archives-experience/charters/constitution.html

Epstein, David. (2006, Feb. 22). When Freedom Isn't Freedom At All. *Inside Higher Ed*. Retrieved July 7, 2006 from http://www.insidehighered.com/news/2006/02/22/supreme

First Amendment Annotations. (2006). [Electronic Version]. Retrieved July 7, 2006 from http://caselaw.lp.findlaw.com/data/constitution/amendment01/

First Amendment Schools. (2004). *How Do Courts Determine if Speech is a True Threat?* [Electronic Version]. Retrieved July 7, 2006 from http://www.firstamendmentschools.org//freedoms/faq.aspx?id=12996&SearchString=true_threat

Fuson, H.W., Jr. (1995). *Telling It All: A Legal Guide to the Exercise of Free Speech*. Kansas City, Mo.: Andrews and McMeel.

Grossman, J. (2001). *Writ*. [Electronic Version]. Retrieved July 7, 2006 from http://writ.news.findlaw.com/grossman/20010213.html

Jaschik, S. (2006, April 17). Setting the Rules on Free Expression. *Inside Higher Ed*. Retrieved July 7, 2006 from http://www.insidehighered.com/news/2006/04/17/ark

Monk, L.R. (1991). *The Bill of Rights: A User's Guide*. Alexandria, VA. Close Up Publishing.

Office for Civil Rights, Department of Education. (2001). *Revised Sexual Harassment Guidance: Harassment of Student by School Employees, Other Students or Third Parties* [Electronic Version]. Retrieved July 7, 2006 from http://www.ed.gov/legislation/FedRegister/other/2001-1/011901b.html

Office for Civil Rights, Department of Education. (2003, July 28). *First Amendment: Dear Colleague* [Electronic version]. Retrieved July 6, 2006 from http://www.ed.gov/about/offices/list/ocr/firstamend.html

Pavela, G. (2004, Jan. 26). Lawful Limits on Freedom of Expression, Synfax Weekly Report. (Available from College Administration Publications, Inc, 830-D Fairview Road, Asheville, NC 28803-1081)

Pavela, G. (2006, May 11). ASJA Law and Policy Report. Number 218. [Electronic Version]. Retrieved July 7, 2006 from http://www.asjaonline.org/

Regents Approve Policy to Guide Resident Assistant Activities on Campus. (2006, March 10). [Electronic Version]. University of Wisconsin System Press Release. Retrieved July 7, 2006 from http://www.wisconsin.edu/news/2006/r060310.htm

Religious Liberty Vindicated Across University of Wisconsin System. (2006, March 14). [Electronic Version]. Foundation for Individual Rights in Education Press Release. Retrieved July 7, 2006 from http://www.thefire.org/index.php/article/6899.html

Texas A&M University. (2006). Texas A&M University Student Code of Conduct [Electronic Version]. Retrieved July 7, 2006 from http://student-rules.tamu.edu/rule24.htm

Wasserman, H. (2004). Fan Profanity. [Electronic Version]. Retrieved July 7, 2006 from http://www.firstamendmentcenter. org/speech/pubcollege/topic.aspx?topic=fan_profanity&Search String=wasserman

CASES REFERENCED

Brandenburg v. Ohio, 395 U.S. 444 (1969)

Bowman v. White 444 F.3d 967 (2006)

Chaplinsky v. New Hampshire, 315 U.S. 568 (1942)

Cohen v. California, 403 U.S. 15 (1971)

Davis v. Monroe County Bd. of Educ., 526 U.S. 629 (1999)

Gay Alliance of Students v. Matthews, 544 F.2d 162 (4th Cir. 1976)

Gay Lib v. University of Missouri, 558 F.2d 848 (8th Cir. 1977)

Gay Student Services v. Texas A&M, 737 F.2d 1317 (5th Cir. 1984)

Hayut v. SUNY New Paltz, et al., 352 F.3d 733 (2d Cir. 2003)

Healy v. James, 408 U.S. 169 (1972)

Hosty v. Carter, 412 F.3d 731 (2005)

Iota Xi Chapter of Sigma Chi Fraternity v. George Mason University, 993 F.2d 386 (1993)

Justice for All v. Faulkner, 410 F.3d 760 (5th Cir. 2005)

Kovacs v. Cooper, 336 U.S. 77 (1949)

Miller v. California, 413 U.S. 15 (1973)

Papish v. Board of Curators of the University of Missouri, 410 U.S. 667 (1973)

Planned Parenthood v. American Coalition of Life Activists, 290 F.3d 1058 (9th Cir. 2002)

Robinson v. California, 370 U.S. 660 (1962)

Rosenberger v. University of Virginia, 515 U.S. 819 (1995)

Tinker v. Des Moines Independent School District, 393 U.S. 503, 506 (1969)

University of Wisconsin v. Southworth, 529 U.S. 217 (2000)

Watts v. U.S., 394 U.S. 705 (1969)

West Virginia State Bd. of Ed. v. Barnette, 319 U.S. 624 (1943)

Wisconsin v. Mitchell, 508 U.S. 47 (1993)

CHAPTER SIX

Practical and Political Realities of a First Amendment Crisis

"The First Amendment is often inconvenient. But that is beside the point. Inconvenience does not absolve the government of its obligation to tolerate speech."

Justice Anthony Kennedy

CHAPTER SIX

IMPACT ON THE COMMUNITY

Seldom is an issue on American college campuses more heated and intense than one related to free speech. American citizens hold dearly to their constitutional rights and naturally fight any efforts to have them taken away. At the same time, as residents of a global community as well as a campus community, administrators strive to practice and teach civility toward one another. Oftentimes these ideals clash violently, and rarely does anyone agree on what takes precedence.

In addition, free speech issues on campus can be the most emotionally draining and painful situations imaginable, while at the same time providing the greatest opportunities for thought, dialogue, debate, and learning. In many ways, such incidents bring out the best of the true ideals of higher education.

The nature of serious free speech conflicts is that they progress rapidly and often reach fever pitch before administrators fully comprehend the incident and its ramifications. Because such incidents involve beliefs and values that are so deeply held, passions and emotions will likely run high.

Although the long-term effects of such conflicts may ultimately have positive outcomes, the process of working through the turmoil can be difficult. It may often seem that administrators are between the proverbial rock and a hard place, given that the choices available are virtually guaranteed to anger someone. Additionally, such decisions, as well as the decision making process, will be continually in the spotlight. Rarely will critics have all of the facts (nor may they want to), and an administrator's words and actions may often be taken out of context and held up on public display to prove the point of one group or another.

Depending on the situation, as well as the history and mission of the specific campus involved, the actions and reactions of the campus may vary widely. As soon as the incident becomes public, it is typical that rumors will abound. As with most perceived and real crises, everyone who becomes aware of the incident (now much faster with the Internet), will have an opinion about the incident and how the administration should respond. Faculty, staff, students, alumni, parents, regents, legislators, donors, and members of the local community may all weigh in on the matter. One of the first critical decisions facing the administration is whether to wait and see what constituents may hear, see, and comment about or decide instead to proactively inform them of the incident (at least what is known at the time) and request their assistance. The authors strongly suggest the latter approach if possible.

The first approach leaves to chance what people on campus and off communicate or understand about the incident. Because communication on most campuses is "spotty" at best, rumors and hearsay can generate more rumors and hearsay. It is well known in crisis management circles that giving people accurate information at regular intervals aids communication and lessens anxiety. Leaders representing the groups mentioned above can greatly help the institution by listening carefully to their peers and constituents and making administrators aware of rumors and rumblings. They can keep a finger on the pulse of the campus and relate critical information necessary for decision making back to the administration. With their close proximity to students, student affairs staff can play a critical role in providing timely information to the administration and communicating information from the administration to students and student leaders. On campuses where trust and communication are generally strong, this is a fairly easy task. Where trust and administrative confidence is generally low, this will seem like an uphill battle. Unfortunately, campuses will likely have their fair share of armchair quarterbacks who, rather than work to ease tensions and offer real assistance, feel compelled to give advice publicly and privately. Press coverage will play a pivotal role in determining the scope of the crisis, which is why it is so critical to create media responses early. It is surprising how fast a campus story can become national news.

Alumni and donors who feel strong ties to the university may threaten to withdraw contributions or support based on actions (or perceived inaction) taken by the university. Decision making by poll watching is dangerous at best; however, creating methods of logging e-mails early on will help the administration track the success of their communication during and after the crisis. Decisions should be based on the incident itself, rather than on early reactions to the incident by various constituent groups.

In cases where the First Amendment crisis deals with a racial incident, communication and decision making tends to be even more challenging. For example, if the mission of the institution states the desire for the university to be a "diverse and inclusive campus," yet does not immediately suspend an individual or group that acts in a clearly racist yet constitutionally protected manner, the campus community will question the administration's commitment to its mission. Likewise, if institutional statements imply that racism will not be tolerated yet the institution seems to do nothing when an incident takes place, campus constituents may be equally confused. Some people will naturally assume that "no tolerance" means taking immediate punitive action. The media, who should be the first to uphold the First Amendment, will latch onto such apparent discrepancies, adding fuel to the fire. There may be a host of vigils and protests scheduled by all sides with the potential to cause further disruption to the campus. Through it all, everyone will have opportunities to learn from the actions of others, while, for the institution, there will be a chance to reaffirm its commitment to preserving a strong diverse campus community while upholding the First Amendment.

External groups and agencies such as the National Association for the Advancement of Colored People (NAACP), the American Civil Liberties Union (ACLU), the National Gay and Lesbian Task Force (NGLTF), or other similar advocacy groups may become involved in campus issues. They can be particularly effective in helping foster the dialogue and bringing disparate members of the community together.

The unfortunate reality is that free speech issues on any campus are typically emotionally intense maelstroms. They will probably be fraught with anger, hurt, divisiveness, and criticism of the campus administrators trying to handle them. There really is no way to please everyone involved, and, as a result, some individuals and groups may feel marginalized and offended. Honoring the law is the right thing to do even in the face of such adversity and controversy.

CREATING A PLAN OF ACTION

Some of these negative effects can at least be minimized with swift and thoughtful action by campus administrators. Although each situation will best be served with individually tailored responses, the following general strategies may prove to be effective:

★ As soon as administrators know about a free speech issue, a response team should be formed. Such a team could include student affairs staff, police or security, appropriate academic affairs staff, legal counsel, and the institution's chief information officer, among others. Although the issue may not blossom, it is much better to be prepared.

★ Begin an investigation immediately, gather as much information as possible, and make a decision as to whether or not the conduct is actionable under state or federal law or through the campus code of conduct. If not, the institution will want to explain its rationale.

★ Respond publicly to the incident as soon as possible. Even when all the facts may not yet be analyzed, it is important to publicly acknowledge awareness of the incident and concern for all involved.

★ Establish methods for "taking the pulse of the campus." Ensure that there is a way to gather all relevant information about events, media coverage, campus concerns, and any responses or actions related to the incident.

★ Determine the three most important messages that the campus wants to send about this incident and make sure that all team members are on the same page. No matter what other fallout occurs in the days ahead, it will be important for the institution to have a consistent message based on its values. (It is useful to remember that one important value may be an unwavering support for individual rights granted by the Constitution.)

★ Determine who will serve as spokespersons for the university and funnel all requests for communication to such spokespersons.

★ Resist the urge to silence any protests, media reports, or other free speech resulting from this incident. Instead, take the lead in inviting campus dialogue about the incident.

★ Encourage faculty and staff to also initiate dialogue about the incident. Such dialogue not only helps people to process the incident, but it can also provide a tremendous learning experience, which is one of the primary goals of any institution of higher education.

★ Establish a regular meeting for the response team. In the midst of a crisis, it may be necessary to meet at least daily.

★ Establish a communication protocol for the response team between meetings so that all information is kept current.

★ Consider establishing a hotline or e-mail address so that the general public can provide input and the institution can confirm facts or deny rumors.

★ Make arrangements for administrators to visit with the affected parties as soon as possible. This could include individual students and faculty as well as campus groups.

★ If individual students were involved in the incident, make sure that a designee meets with them and that their safety needs are being addressed.

★ Help involved students or student leaders understand how best to interact with the media.

★ If a student organization involved in the incident has a national organization, notify the national office immediately.

★ Political action groups may demand that "heads roll" for an incident. Take such demands into the same consideration as any other advice provided and resist acting from pressure rather than from analysis and thought.

If disciplinary action is warranted:

★ Proceed according to policies and procedures and base decision making on evidence.

★ Investigate all allegations thoroughly. Focus on behavior.

★ Consider the totality of the circumstances and apply a reasonable person standard in determining if it is more likely than not that a violation of the code or policy occurred.

★ As Judge Alfred Murrah said, "Hear the case before you decide it."

★ Consult with institutional legal counsel.

★ Avoid making a First Amendment martyr out of a perpetrator.

In short, the institution needs to realize that the incident has already taken place and cannot be changed. What administrators can do, however, is to be powerful in asserting the mission, caring for the community, and inviting free exploration of the world of ideas.

Dealing With The Media

A "no holds barred" free speech crisis on a college campus is the stuff that dreams are made of for members of the media. Such incidents tend to draw intense emotional and vocal participants and the kinds of vigils and protests that seem tailor-made for news clips. Something about the idea of such a violent clash of values on the grounds where learning takes place invites public voyeurism. In addition, the very idea that anyone's constitutional rights could be trampled in this country may cause even the most mild-mannered citizen to react with outrage. Emotions are high, everyone seems to be involved, and values are put on the line. What could possibly make for a better story?

The challenge, then, is to find a way to manage all of the media requests while sending a consistent message about what the institution stands for. Given that any message will be interpreted in many different ways by those who hear it, administrators should carefully craft and send such messages via the media.

In the best case scenario, the institution will have a chief information officer and/or staff that can provide valuable assistance in directing these efforts. Even so, individual administrators may find themselves in a media situation that requires a response without such assistance on hand. In any event, the following suggestions for working with the media may help to craft the messages and limit their chances for misinterpretation:

★ Know with certainty that the media will attempt to tell the story with or without assistance. It is okay to state that the university is investigating the incident and will respond as information is available. It is not recommended to talk around the issue or guess with members of the media.

★ The campus will be featured on the news. The choice is to either help the media tell the story or allow it to be told as the media see it.

★ Determine three important messages that are intended for the community and focus answers or comments on these. Plan what to communicate and prepare for questions that may be asked.

★ Avoid being pressured by the media's sense of urgency. Take time to write and answer three or four anticipated questions.

★ Identify one or two spokespersons for the university. Be sure they are not only informed about the incident but also about the process for dealing with campus incidents in general.

★ Drive the train to avoid being hit by it! Craft thoughtful responses for the campus community. Involve as many campus and community leaders as early as possible.

★ Consider holding a press conference; but keep in mind that if not properly controlled, this can be a difficult venture. Begin by stating the message(s) and be prepared for any questions that might be asked.

★ Consider distributing frequent press releases with up-to-date information.

★ Do not say anything not intended to be published or broadcast.

★ Respond to media requests as soon as possible, and do not appear to be hiding from the media.

★ Avoid a defensive response.

★ Tell the truth.

★ Be prepared to say, "I don't know" or, "We are still determining that." ("No comment" will attract media scrutiny.)

★ Talk about what the institution is doing.

★ Frame things as positively as possible. Rather than saying, "The law won't allow us to punish them," talk about the institution's commitment to upholding the individual rights guaranteed in the Constitution. At the same time, it is possible to condemn the hurt that some people have caused and to remind the media that such incivility is not part of the institution's values. The most important part of the statement should always be concern for the people involved.

★ Feel free to have notes to reference with the important discussion points.

★ Ask a trusted colleague to role play an interview before actually meeting with the media.

★ Be cordial and polite to all members of the media and avoid assumptions of mistrust.

★ Be clear and direct with answers. There is no need to provide long-winded explanations, which may increase the chance of being misquoted.

PRACTICAL APPLICATION

Although there are many principles and precedents to guide administrative action in incidents related to free speech, seldom will an event lend itself to a single easy resolution. Instead, various perspectives and approaches may need to be blended with the nature of the specific incident and the culture of the campus. In addition, any free speech issue on campus will likely blossom quickly, with the campus finding itself in the center of controversy, media attention, and opinions, including criticisms.

Given the potential for crisis, it is wise for any institution to plan ahead to the extent possible, by discussing various scenarios and responses. Proactive planning will provide initial guidelines and thoughts when an incident does occur.

An identical scenario may be perceived differently on two campuses, depending on considerations such as campus climate, history, and mission, to name a few. No matter what kind of campus or what the incidence is, it is helpful to immediately identify the most important issues and to proactively chart a course of action based on variables specific to the individual campus. The action plan below may be useful when creating the course of action. The plan can be completed by one person but will probably be more effective when used by a campus response team.

CAMPUS ACTION PLAN

1. Whose safety or welfare is of immediate concern and what needs to be done about it right now?

Who	What Needs to Be Done	Who Will Do It

2. Who needs to be notified (internally and externally) of what?

Who Needs to be Notified	Of What	Who Will Do It

3. What information do we need and how will we obtain it?

4. Who needs to be part of the initial response team?

5. What messages do we want to send?

Message	Intended Audience	Method of Communication

6. Who will serve as media contacts for the university?

7. Is this incident actionable in any way?

8. Who are our primary stakeholders and how are they likely to respond?

Stakeholder	Interest/Issue/Need	Action or Communication Needed	Person Responsible

9. How does our institutional mission affect our response to this incident?

10. How will we systematically gather feedback/responses to this incident?

11. Is there campus history/culture that is relevant to this event?

12. Have there been similar incidents on other campuses that might be instructive to the administration?

13. How does the current campus climate affect this situation?

14. What campus policies are relevant to this situation?

15. What resources are available to the institution as we deal with this incident?

16. What else do we anticipate happening as a result of this incident and how do we plan for it?

17. What other issues/concerns/needs could result from this incident?

Case Study Using the Campus Action Plan

As each campus and incident may differ significantly, responses to items on the action plan may also vary. With practiced use of the plan, administrators may begin to think more broadly about the wide-reaching implications of both the event as well as possible institutional responses.

In order to consider the use of such a plan, imagine the following scenario, which was described earlier:

ABC Fraternity—Case Study

A fraternity sponsored and hosted a costume party off campus with invited guests and dates. One member dressed as a Klansman and pretended to hang a man in blackface wearing a prisoner's uniform. A third man held a bullwhip above the head of the "prisoner." These behaviors, immortalized on film, were available for purchase on the hired photographer's Web site protected by the super-secret access password, "Greek." The site was reported to Tolerance.org, a branch of the Southern Poverty Law Center.

You are the vice president for student affairs at a large, public university with a predominately Caucasian enrollment. The Greek Life coordinator stops by your office to let you know about the incident and that Tolerance.org has called him for comments. It is unclear how Tolerance.org received the information and what other groups or individuals (internal or external to the university) may know about the incident at this time.

Your secretary informs you that a representative from Tolerance.org is on line 1 and the president of the African American Student Association is on line 2.

After speaking with both parties, you realize just how complex this incident is and begin the process of gathering information. As you do so, you realize that information (and misinformation) about the incident is spreading rapidly across campus.

The Media Frenzy Begins

In the days and weeks that follow an incident such as this, campus, community, regional, and state media outlets will weigh in on what the university is doing or should be doing to address the incident. The campus will likely be deluged with e-mails from students, parents, alumni, and others that represent a continuum of emotions and opinions about the incident and the institution's response. The following are actual excerpts from campus and area media sources and e-mails sent to the Oklahoma State University administration regarding this particular incident.

"Black Students Outraged: Students Demand Action at Afro-Am Meeting" by Rachel Richardson, staff writer, *The Daily O'Collegian*, Sept. 27, 2002

"...Some say it's free speech," Clark (Afro-Am President) said. "I think differently. I don't want to pry into anybody's free speech but if you are going to be a fraternity at OSU, that should not be tolerated. Clark challenged the OSU administration to "follow their policy of having no tolerance."

Letter to the administration

"...It's up to you, the administrators to take an unequivocal stand against the hate and intolerance that such action promotes. You must find the moral backbones to convincingly distinguish between protecting free speech and protecting hate. Much posturing and empty rhetoric will not get it."

"Good Ole' Boys at OSU" by Scott Byrd, *The Daily O'Collegian*, Sept. 27, 2002

"...so what can be done about this act of hatred? How can this injustice be righted? Will our university take a leadership role in delivering a penalty or will they just take care of it behind closed doors?"

"... Last year at Auburn University students were indefinitely suspended and two fraternity houses were closed after students wore a KKK [Ku Klux Klan] costume and blackface to fraternity Halloween parties. Also, last year a fraternity house at Ole' Miss was suspended for the same thing."

"Stupid," *Tulsa World* editorial, Sept. 30, 2002

"...The problem is that once something like this gets out of the gate, there's no getting it back in. The damage is done and all the explanations and apologies ring hollow."

Statement from the editorial board, *The Daily O'Collegian*, Sept. 26, 2002

"...Swift action needs to be taken on the part of the university and others involved with the Greek system. Allowing this type of behavior to go unpunished any significant amount of time will only make the university look worse. An apology after being caught does not constitute reparations for an act or acknowledgement of the audacity of an act. It only represents immaturity and fear of consequences—not knowledge of the audacity of guilt."

"Greek Party a Display of Stupidity" by C. Brooks Kurts, *The Daily O'Collegian*, Sept. 27, 2002

"...so now that the obvious has been pointed out, what is State University to do? What is AGR Fraternity to do? On OSU's end there is obviously a conflict. First, this was a private party. Second, free speech—even really stupid free speech—is protected, especially in private. On the other end of it, though, if they don't do something along the lines of kicking the house off-campus, it's going to make OSU look like a bunch of cracker-toting bigots..."

"Not All AGRs are Guilty of Hate," Letter to the editor, *The Daily O'Collegian*, Sept. 30, 2002

"...the opinions expressed by opinion columnists and statements in articles have encouraged people to believe that the entire AGR membership are stupid rednecks who hate African-Americans. This is unfair. I am amazed that the positive impact and the contributions that this outstanding fraternity has made to State University, the City and State, can be completely forgotten because of the inappropriate actions of a few individuals."

Letter to the editor by Chris Jenkins, *The Daily O'Collegian*, Oct. 1, 2002

"...I applaud the paper for its coverage of the issue, but I ask the university, as well as the Greek System as a whole, enough with the damage control, lies and lip service."

Letter to the President, Oct. 3, 2002

"It amazes me that a university accepts exclusive all-black fraternities and sororities, allows Preacher Bob to call women sluts and whores on campus property, and says 'freedom of speech' when international students protest against the United States on campus has now set itself as the watchdog to protect the student body against 'insensitive actions' regarding off-campus activity by students."

Change Only Comes with Action by Steven Hunt, *The Daily O'Collegian*, Oct. 2, 2002

"This group has been caught in a situation presenting members as people who could cause real danger to another group. The current philosophy in our land, if I am not mistaken, is that when such evidence arises—a threat is presented by a people—then the right thing to do is eliminate them.

"...A fraternity recruitment [brochure] states: All but two U.S. presidents since 1825, 100 of the 158 cabinet members since 1908, 76% of current U.S. Senators and Congress members and about 80% of the top executives of Fortune 500 companies have been fraternity men.

"One only needs to look at the number of black people in these positions and know how things are and what must be subtly done by their oppressors to maintain these things."

Given this scenario and early reactions to the incident, how might your campus begin to resolve this First Amendment crisis? Because each campus is different with a unique history and culture, decisions are likely to be different in every case. The following action plan reflects how one campus responded.

EXAMPLE OF A COMPLETED CAMPUS ACTION PLAN

1. Whose safety or welfare is of immediate concern, and what needs to be done about it right now?

Who	What Needs to Be Done	Who Will Do It
ABC Fraternity leadership	Notify them of the current publicity and initial response and concern for their safety. Instruct them to direct media calls to the university public information officer and pay attention to house security measures.	Greek life coordinator Vice president for student affairs
African-American students	Notify leadership of incident and offer any assistance needed. Provide them with administrator emergency contact information.	Vice president for student affairs Greek life coordinator Academic vice president

2. Who needs to be notified (internally and externally) of what?

Who Needs to Be Notified	Of What	Who Will Do It
University president	Tolerance.org Web site, nature of calls received, and any actions taken	Vice president for student affairs
University Board of Regents	Tolerance.org Web site, reactions of campus constituents to date, and the position of the university on this issue and next steps to be taken by the university	President
Campus and city police	Safety concerns for the fraternity involved and its members, the possibility of vandalism against the frat house, and possible demonstrations/vigils on or off campus	Vice president for student affairs
Public information officer	Incident details known at the time; the position of the university that this is protected speech; desired response by the university, including condemnation of the actions of the fraternity involved	Vice president for student affairs
Executive team	Awareness of incident and possible reactions, identify spokesperson(s) for university	Vice president for student affairs or president
African American student leadership	Web site, Tolerance.org inquiry, and any safety concerns	Vice president for student affairs
ABC Fraternity national office	Inform them of incident and request their assistance locally	Vice president for student affairs and Greek life staff

153

3. What information do we need and how will we obtain it?

★   More information about the party (i.e., purpose, location, size, alcohol use). Obtain information from Greek coordinator, ABC Fraternity president, and social chair.

★   Who attended the party (i.e., fraternity members, guests)?

★   Who took the pictures? How do we get them off the party-pic Web site (contact company)?

★   What is the initial reaction of African Americans? Contact the African American leadership.

4. Who needs to be part of the initial response team?

★   President

★   Vice presidents (i.e., vice president for student affairs, academic affairs)

★   Legal representative for the university

★   Public information director

★   Greek life coordinator

★   Campus police chief

5. What messages do we want to send?

Message	Intended Audience	Method of Communication
"We are shocked and appalled by the pictures on the Web."	Community	TV, paper, e-mail blast if available, university homepage
"We are investigating the incident fully."	Faculty, staff, students, alumni, general community	TV, paper, e-mail blast if available, university homepage
"We support the First Amendment rights of students even when their judgment and actions are morally reprehensible."	Faculty, staff, students, alumni, general community	TV, paper, e-mail blast if available, university homepage
"We remain committed to diversity and civility and will work to heal the wounds this incident has created."	Faculty, staff, students, alumni, general community	TV, paper, e-mail blast if available, university homepage

6. Who will serve as media contacts for the university?

After discussing the incident fully, it is determined that three people will speak on behalf of the university—the president, vice president for student affairs, and the public information officer. Others will update and advise the spokespersons. They were selected based on prior experience with the media and knowledge about campus policies and procedures.

7. Is this incident actionable in any way?

It has been determined that this racist incident is not actionable under the student code of conduct and, while despicable, is protected symbolic speech. However, the IFC can address possible violations of its policies (non-state action). Complaints will be written to the IFC.

Alcohol use by those pictured (who were underage) may be addressed by the IFC or the university or both.

8. Who are our primary stakeholders and how are they likely to respond?

Stakeholder	Interest/Issue/Need	Action or Communication Needed	Person Responsible
African American Student Association	Feelings of anger, isolation, fear, and uncertainty. They will want to know what steps are being considered or taken by the university. They may need guidance on how to deal with the media and how to craft meaningful messages to the fraternity involved.	Meet with African American leadership and members to listen to concerns, discuss what is known about the incident to date, possible action steps the university is considering.	President and vice president for student affairs, if possible
Faculty of Color Black Alumni Association	They need facts and initial thoughts on possible university actions to be taken. They may ask how they can support students of color on campus. May discuss the need for mandatory classes dealing with diversity.	Meet with leadership of both groups and inform them of the facts known at this time.	Vice president for student affairs, provost, or president

Stakeholder	Interest/Issue/Need	Action or Communication Needed	Person Responsible
Faculty council	They need facts and initial thoughts on possible university actions to be taken. They may ask how they can support students of color on campus. May discuss the need for mandatory classes dealing with diversity.	Meet with leadership of group and inform them of facts known at this time.	Vice president for student affairs, provost, or president
Student Government Association	Facts about the incident, what they can do to help, how to respond to media inquiries	Meet with student leaders to share information and discuss media inquiries.	Vice president for student affairs, public information officer
Greek Life	Facts that are known at this time and potential impact on the house involved and Greek system as a whole	Share information and discuss media requests.	Vice president for student affairs and Greek Life coordinator
Alumni/donors	They need facts and initial thoughts on possible university actions to be taken. They may ask how they can support students of color on campus.	Meet with leadership of group and inform them of facts known at this time.	

9. How does our institutional mission affect our response to this incident?

Increasing diversity (faculty, staff, and students) is part of our strategic plan, initiative, and mission. We train to prevent racial and sexual harassment.

10. How will we systematically gather feedback/responses to this incident?

We will set up a clipping agency or recruit staff volunteers to review articles from selected newspapers. Identify two to three people who can respond to e-mail communications and letters and log and sort all communication.

11. Is there campus history/culture that is relevant to this event?

Yes, incidents in 1965 resulted in a two-day boycott of classes following a racial incident on campus.

12. Have there been similar incidents on other campuses that might be instructive to the administration?

George Mason University, Auburn University, and Ole' Miss have had similar incidents on campus. The vice president of student affairs instructed to work with legal counsel to research similar cases and outcomes. It is discovered that, while the universities involved opted to suspend fraternities for symbolic speech, the courts overturned the findings and reinstated the fraternities.

13. How does the current campus climate affect this situation?

★ Campus protests likely

★ Uneasiness due to 9/11 impact

14. What campus policies are relevant to this situation?

★ IFC policies regarding image, conduct, and underage alcohol use

★ University code of conduct regarding alcohol use by minors

15. What resources are available to the institution as we deal with this incident?

★ The OCR, Justice Department, and the NAACP have contacted the university and are willing to help the university if necessary.

★ Knowledgeable faculty and staff can educate fraternity members and other students about racism.

★ There is a willingness and opportunity for hosting campus forums/vigils.

★ Leaders of affected groups have an opportunity to meet together with president and other administrators to discuss ways to help heal the community.

16. What else do we anticipate happening as a result of this incident and how do we plan for it?

★ Bad press is likely both locally and nationally. We will need to continue to tell our story and update media on self-imposed, nationally imposed, and IFC-imposed sanctions.

★ Vigils and protests may occur.

★ We anticipate that there will be calls to suspend the fraternity.

★ Greater media attention may be disruptive.

★ Anniversary of the event may be significant in the future.

★ Violence against fraternity members or fraternity house is possible.

17. What other issues/concerns/needs could result from this incident?

★ This incident may affect minority recruitment and retention.

★ Curricular change discussions will likely take place.

★ Effect on Greek system is uncertain.

CHAPTER SEVEN

Healing Communities and Stakeholders

*The very reason for the First Amendment
is to make the people of this country free
to think, speak, write and worship as they
wish, not as the Government commands.*

Justice Hugo L. Black

There is no question that an intense free speech controversy on campus can cause great pain, anger, mistrust, criticism, and feelings of oppression. Indeed, history shows us that numerous campuses have suffered through that and more.

For an administrator, initial crisis management truly is just the tip of the iceberg. Throughout the crisis and for some time afterward, the wounds will remain open and the pain will maintain its intensity. There will be those who still disagree with the action or inaction of the institution, those who feel victimized, those who feel silenced, and those who feel that their viewpoints and emotions were not considered. Although it is up to the entire community to engage in the healing process, campus officials tend to have the most authority, opportunity, and resources to direct this process.

AT THE ONSET OF THE INCIDENT

Although it is inevitable that a campus administration will be criticized no matter what formal action is taken or not taken, it is important to always focus foremost on the safety and well-being of the individuals most directly involved. Threats toward the alleged perpetrators are not uncommon. From the very beginning, it is important to continually try to identify those who may be experiencing a negative impact from the incident and to provide as much institutional support as possible. This may include meeting with students or groups who were affected by the speech to assess their welfare, listen to their issues, offer campus support sources, inform them about the institution's plans for action, and simply let them know that their concerns are being heard. The needs of faculty and staff should also receive close attention.

162

It is critical for administrators to gather as much information as possible and to determine whether or not disciplinary action can be taken against any individual or group involved. **In reality, most campus free-speech controversies involve protected speech.** Many members of the community will not understand this, however, when they feel frustrated and angry. Thus, it will be important for the institution to provide a thoughtful rationale to the public if the decision has been made to not take formal disciplinary action.

Most institutions would assert that they not only care deeply for their students and staff, but that they also value diversity, civility, and positive citizenship. Given those claims, it is understandable that so many wonder with incredulity why the administration is not punishing the offenders and making strong public statements against their inappropriate or hateful expression. Administrators also want to uphold and honor the First Amendment. It is at those times that administrators can feel caught in the middle. In addition, it can be difficult for administrators to put their own personal values and feelings about the situation aside in order to uphold the law. Doing what is legally the "right thing" may indeed seem quite difficult.

It is possible to condemn hurtful or hateful expression without taking formal disciplinary action(s). The campus community should be encouraged to express its outrage and hurt in a civil and appropriate manner. This will have the most impact when it comes from high-ranking administrators. It will be powerful to hear a university president say, "Although this institution will always uphold persons' rights to lawfully express themselves, I am truly disappointed and appalled that members of our community would hurt other members in such a way."

Kenneth Stern, attorney and nationally recognized expert on American hate groups, stated:

As any administration official who has had to do it can attest, responding to an incident is a complex affair. Passions are high, and each incident has a new wrinkle not previously thought through. The institution's view of itself and its commitment to free speech are challenged.

The most important rule is the simplest to effectuate. When an incident occurs, the university, at its highest level, must respond immediately and strongly. Presidents must make themselves as public as possible, and say—in the most powerful words—that bigotry has no place on campus. Period.

Failure to act quickly with a clear statement will create an escalating crisis. Wishy-washy, delayed, or low level pronouncements say that bigotry is not a serious problem and that the hurt students feel is somehow invalid. That invites further and longer explosions. (Stern, 2000, p. 7)

Hearing such a message from the president, from other administrators, and from student leaders can serve as an affirmation to aggrieved students. It can be delivered through the media, to students through mass e-mail communication, and in public at forums or vigils and small group and one-on-one sessions as time permits. Having the university plan and sponsor such events as soon as possible, rather than waiting for students to take the lead, sends the message even more directly.

It is also important to meet directly with the individuals or group that engaged in the expression and caused the controversy. They are doubtless the recipients of much negative attention, and their welfare and safety must also be of concern. The campus may be able to provide them with assistance in dealing with the media, as well as advice and/or support for dealing with their own personal safety.

In The Weeks That Follow

The intensity of such an incident may last for several weeks as new information becomes available, related events unfold, and the media remains involved. During this time, it is certainly important to maintain all of the actions initiated at the onset of the crisis, but special attention must also be paid as new issues emerge.

Ideally, administrators have already established the messages that the campus wants to send through the media, and those messages should continue to focus on the safety, dignity, and well-being of the campus community, as well as condemnation of the incivility involved. As related events such as vigils, protests, and forums evolve, institutional calls for greater diversity and diversity education will be intense.

Campus administrators and faculty should attend events such as forums and vigils to demonstrate support for the community, as well as the issues raised. Each venue offers an opportunity for the institution to reaffirm its commitment to core values and condemn an environment of incivility. As unpopular as it may be at first, the college or university also needs to affirm its commitment to the First Amendment, which should also be addressed as a core value. Attendance at such events offers a chance for staff members to spend individual time with students to assess their welfare. Finally, it provides the best opportunity to monitor the pulse of the campus.

It will be critical to maintain contact with the individual(s) or group that began the controversy to help them understand the impact of their actions and the institution's feelings about their conduct. This will become especially important as events unfold and perpetrators find themselves the center of attention. Remember that the majority of campus free-speech incidents have been launched by people who act unwittingly and who are oblivious to the amount of hurt they will cause. Once this becomes apparent, many such offenders are eager to apologize and attempt to make amends to the community. At this point in time, assistance from campus officials to direct and reinforce their efforts will be helpful.

During times of intense emotion and conflict, people want to feel that they are being heard and that the institution cares about their opinions. Although personal appearances offer one way to do this, they cannot meet the needs of everyone who wants to express an opinion. It may also be helpful to set up alternate methods of communication such as a hotline or Web site. This provides another way to monitor feelings about the incident and allows the institution to track comments. It is critical, of course, that someone read and respond to such comments in a timely manner. Thoughtful and personal correspondence remains the best tool of communication.

THE AFTERMATH

No one would want to live through such a painful series of events without having somehow grown stronger through the process. Therefore, it is crucial that the event, as well as the community's response, become part of the institution's history. It is important for the entire campus community to assess how the environment contributed to the incident and how respect can be fostered in the future. Administrators can facilitate this process by initiating task forces and reviews, examining how institutional values affect the community and reviewing the institution's response to the situation. Of course, in order for these actions to be a learning process, they must involve a cross-section of the community, and outcomes should be reported back to all members of the community.

It is also critical to continue to support the community, as people will feel emotional about the event long after the whirlwind of the crisis has passed. An astute response team will plan proactively to meet with affected groups at periodic intervals in the future. Such discussions will reaffirm the institution's concern for all and will provide helpful feedback at a time when emotions have calmed, and participants have had the chance to process the incident.

In addition, the classroom can be a good place for learning from the scenario. Faculty can be encouraged to infuse issues such as First Amendment rights, community civility, citizenship, bigotry, and other related issues into their curricula.

Any campus community that has gone through such an incident will most certainly have grown stronger in many ways as a result. The ability to identify those strengths and determine how to utilize them positively in the future will also serve as a great healer.

CHAPTER SEVEN

BIBLIOGRAPHY

Stern, K. (2000). *Bigotry on Campus: A Planned Response.* New York, NY: American Jewish Committee.

168

CHAPTER EIGHT

Important Cases Related to Free Speech On Campus

"The very purpose of a Bill of Rights was to withdraw certain subjects from the vicissitudes of political controversy, to place them beyond the reach of majorities and officials and to establish them as legal principles to be applied by the courts. One's right to life, liberty, and property, to free speech, a free press, freedom of worship and assembly, and other fundamental rights may not be submitted to vote; they depend on the outcome of no elections."

Justice Robert H. Jackson

1. Blair v. Shippensburg University, 280 F. Supp. 2d 357 (M.D. Pa. 2003)

In this case, the Court enjoined enforcement of a university's code of conduct located within its "Racism and Cultural Diversity Policy Statement" because its provisions prohibiting acts of intolerance directed at others and a provision defining racism were overbroad and could be interpreted as prohibiting protected speech. Additionally, the Court noted that a section of the code that directed students to communicate their beliefs in a manner that "does not provoke, harass, intimidate, or harm another" was clearly overbroad and unduly restricted "offensive" speech.

2. Board of Education, Island Trees Union Free School District v. Pico, 457 U.S. 853 (1982)

In *Pico*, the Court dealt with the validity of the practice of "book-banning" in public high school libraries. A plurality of the Court ruled that such a practice would not violate the principles of the First Amendment if the decisive factor in the school's decision to ban the material was based on a good-faith belief that the books were vulgar or otherwise educationally unsuitable rather than a desire "to deny [students] access to ideas with which [the school board] disagreed." In an opinion, which was at times confusing, the Court indicated that while the school could select books at its discretion in the first place, it could not later remove them just to eliminate the dissemination of views it disliked.

3. Board of Regents of the University of Wisconsin System v. Southworth, 529 U.S. 217 (2000)

The Court established that public universities can use a portion of a student's mandatory student fee to fund groups with which a student does not agree as long as the institution does not discriminate based on viewpoint. In *Southworth*, a group of students from the University of Wisconsin argued that their First Amendment rights had been violated by the school's practice of charging each student a mandatory student fee, which was then used to fund various student activities and publications. The money was then distributed by the student government to organizations that it had selected or by a campus referendum in which all students could vote to give money to certain organizations. Several organizations that the group of students objected to received substantial amounts of funds. The litigating students wanted the ability to prevent their money from going to these organizations.

The Supreme Court held that the university system could, without violating the First Amendment rights of the students, charge its students an activity fee used to fund a program to facilitate extracurricular student speech and distribute the money itself. **The Court justified its decision in this case with the logic that the university was exacting "the fee at issue for the sole purpose of facilitating the free and open exchange of ideas by, and among, its students"** *as long* **as it was not discriminating against people of a specific viewpoint.**

4. *Bonnell v. Lorenzo*, 241 F.3d 800 (6th Cir. 2001)

The Court reversed an order for a preliminary injunction granted to a college professor who had been under disciplinary suspension for allegedly violating the community college's sexual harassment policy. The Court noted that "although Plaintiff's speech addressed a matter of public concern, Plaintiff failed to show that his interests in speaking outweighed the College's interests in enforcing its policies."

5. *Booher v. Board of Regents of Northern Kentucky University*, U.S. Dist. LEXIS 11404 (E.D. Ky. 1998)

The Court determined that a university's sexual harassment policy was facially invalid under the First Amendment due to vagueness and overbreadth. The Court noted that the "policy gives one the impression that speech of a sexual nature that is merely offensive would constitute sexual harassment..." This case is highly noteworthy in that it seems to facially reject even codes closely mirroring Equal Employment Opportunity Commission language.

6. *Boy Scouts of America v. Dale,* 530 U.S. 640 (2000)

The Court upheld the Boy Scouts' dismissal of a homosexual scoutmaster, finding that forcing the group to allow a leader who conveyed a message in contradiction with that of the Boy Scouts' official position violated their freedom of association.

7. *Brandenburg v. Ohio*, 395 U.S. 444 (1969)

In *Brandenburg,* the Supreme Court outlined the standard for when words may be considered "incitement" rather than mere speech, and therefore may not be protected under the First Amendment. In that case, a leader of the Ku Klux Klan was convicted under an Ohio statute for threatening that "if our President, our Congress, our Supreme Court continue to suppress the white, Caucasian race, it's possible that there might have to be some revengeance [sic] taken." **The Court held speech that merely *advocates* rather than actually *incites* violence shall be protected by the First Amendment. The Court held that "the constitutional guarantees of free speech and free press do not permit a State to forbid or proscribe advocacy of the use of force or of law violation except where such advocacy is directed** to inciting or producing *imminent lawless action* and is likely to produce such action." [Emphasis ours.]

8. *Capital Square Review and Advisory Board v. Pinette*, 515 U.S. 753 (1995)

The Court allowed the display of a cross by the Ku Klux Klan in a plaza surrounding the Ohio statehouse, noting that private religious speech is **"as fully protected under the Free Speech Clause as secular private expression."** As long as the religious expression is purely private and occurs in a traditional or designated public forum, publicly announced and open to all on equal terms, it does not violate the Establishment Clause.

9. *Chaplinsky v. New Hampshire*, 315 U.S. 568 (1942)

In this case, a man named Chaplinsky was convicted under a state statute for verbally attacking the city marshal by calling him a "damned racketeer" and a "damned Fascist." This case took place during World War II, at a time in which accusations of racketeering or fascism were taken quite seriously. **The Court upheld Chaplinsky's conviction, holding that these epithets were "fighting words," which were "likely to provoke the average person to retaliation, and thereby cause a breach of the peace."**

10. *Chapman v. Thomas*, 743 F.2d 1056 (4th Cir. 1984)

The Court held that the state university's selective solicitation policy was reasonable and not aimed at suppressing a student's religious activities merely because of opposition to his views. The Court found that the dormitories were nonpublic forums, so that a state not only could enforce reasonable time, place, and manner restrictions but also could reserve the forum for its intended purposes (in this case, so-licitation by candidates for student government) as long as the regulation on speech was reasonable and not an effort to suppress expression merely because the state opposed the speaker's view.

11. *Cohen v. California*, 403 U.S. 15 (1971)

In protest against the Vietnam War draft, a man named Cohen wore a jacket bearing the words "Fuck the Draft" into the Los Angeles County Courthouse. He was arrested on the grounds that this was "offensive conduct" that might provoke violence against him. The Supreme Court disagreed, holding that the words on Cohen's jacket were constitutionally protected speech under the First Amendment and that California did not have the power to proscribe the use of such language. Justice John M. Harlan held that Cohen had a right to express his dissatisfaction under the Constitution which "leaves matters of taste and style...**largely to the individual.**" **After all, as Justice Harlan notes, "one man's vulgarity is another's lyric."**

12. *Cohen v. San Bernardino Valley College*, 92 F.3d 968 (9th Cir. 1996)

A professor was punished, based on his teaching methods, under a provision of the college's sexual harassment policy, which prohibits conduct that has the "effect of unreasonably interfering with an individual's academic performance or creating an intimidating, hostile, or offensive learning environment." The Court found that the policy was too vague as applied to the professor because it was used to punish teaching methods that he had been using for many years.

13. *Connick v. Myers,* 461 U.S. 138 (1983)

The Court upheld the discharge of an assistant district attorney who circulated to other assistants a questionnaire concerning office transfer policy, office morale, the need for a grievance committee, confidence in supervisors, and whether employees felt pressured to work in political campaigns. The Court found that it involved matters of personal concern, rather than public concern, which would be of social or political significance to the community and therefore the limited First Amendment interest involved did not require the supervisor to tolerate action which he reasonably believed would disrupt the office, undermine his authority, and destroy close working relationships.

14. *Dambrot v. Central Michigan University,* 55 F.3d 1177 (1993)

Dambrot involved a basketball coach who was fired by the university for using a racial epithet to "motivate" his basketball team. The Court ruled that the university's harassment policy was unconstitutionally broad and vague and was furthermore directed at censoring unpopular viewpoints and, accordingly, prohibited the university from enforcing the policy. However, the Court also held that the coach's use of the epithet in such a context was not a public issue and had no relation to the "marketplace of ideas." Therefore, the coach's constitutional rights were not harmed by the policy in this specific case, and the university had a right to fire him for using that particular speech in the context of his employment.

15. *Davis v. Monroe County Bd. of Educ.,* 526 U.S. 629 (1999)

Davis is the only Supreme Court case to deal with peer-on-peer harassment under Title IX in an educational setting. That case clearly established the analysis for deciding if a pattern of behavior is substantially ratcheted up from the standard that would establish harassment in the employer-employee or faculty-student context.

The analysis prescribed by the Supreme Court requires the conduct in question be sufficiently "severe," "pervasive," *and* "objectionably offensive" to have a "systematic effect" that "effectively bars the victim's access to an educational opportunity or benefit." It also suggests that in evaluating these questions, the "constellation of surrounding circumstances, expectations, and relationships" must be considered.

With regard to severity, the behavior at issue in *Davis* involved repeated groping, fondling, and invasion of personal space to such an extent that the perpetrator was eventually charged with and pleaded guilty to sexual battery. The Court, in fact, specifically noted that in *Davis,* the "harassment was not only verbal; it included numerous acts of objectively offensive touching." *Davis* even stated, "It is thus understandable that, in the school setting, students often engage in insults, banter, teasing, shoving, pushing, and gender-specific conduct that is upsetting to the students subjected to it. **Damages are not available for simple acts of teasing and name-calling** among school children . . ." [Emphasis ours]

It is important to note that *Davis* took place in the context of a public grade school. Since the Supreme Court has found on numerous occasions that the protections of the First Amendment are far greater in a college context and at their lowest ebb in the grade school context, it is hard to imagine the severity of behavior necessary to trigger a finding of actionable peer-to-peer harassment in the higher education context.

16. *Doe v. University of Michigan,* 721 F. Supp. 852 (E.D. Mich., 1989)

In *Doe v. Michigan,* the University of Michigan enacted a discrimination policy that prohibited any verbal or physical behavior that stigmatized or created a "demeaning environment" for others at the school. A graduate student sued the university, claiming that because of the code, he did not feel free to discuss controversial theories about psychology in class. A federal district court agreed, finding that the speech code was overbroad both in the way it was written and in the way it was applied to students, and prohibited the university from continuing to use the code.

17. *Faragher v. City of Boca Raton,* 524 U.S. 775 (1998)

In looking at the standards under Title VII, the Court noted that "conduct must be extreme" to amount to actionable discriminatory harassment so that Title VII does not become a "general civility code." (Furthermore, the Court found that although an employer may be held vicariously liable for actionable discrimination caused by a supervisor, there is an available affirmative defense that looks to the reasonableness of the employer's conduct as well as that of a plaintiff victim.)

18. *Feiner v. New York,* 340 U.S. 315 (1951)

The Court upheld the conviction of a man giving a speech on a street corner because he constituted a clear and present danger. He was arrested after he ignored the requests of police to stop the speech for fear of causing a riot among the angry crowd.

19. *Forsyth County v. Nationalist Movement*, 505 U.S. 123 (1992)

The Court found invalid an ordinance which permitted a government administrator to vary the fee associated with a permit for parades, assemblies, demonstrations, road closings, and other uses of public property and roads by private organizations and groups of private persons for private purposes to reflect the estimated cost of maintaining public order. The Court held that regulations that permit the government to discriminate on the basis of the content of the message cannot be tolerated under the First Amendment and the ordinance unconstitutionally tied the amount of the fee to the content of the speech without providing adequate procedural safeguards.

20. *Gay Student Services v. Texas A&M*, 737 F.2d 1317 (5th Cir. 1984)

The Court found that the university's refusal to recognize a gay student group violated the prohibition against content-based discrimination by the state and therefore violated the group's First Amendment rights. Furthermore, the university could not engage in viewpoint discrimination because it was a limited public forum, and no compelling interest justified its action.

21. *Hague v. Committee for Industrial Organization*, 307 U.S. 496 (1939)

The Court held invalid an ordinance that prohibited public parades or assemblies without a permit because, as drafted, it allowed for arbitrary suppression of speech noting that parks **"have immemorially been held in trust for the use of the public and, time out of** mind, have been used for purposes of assembly, communicating thoughts between citizens, and discussing public questions."

22. *Hardy v. Jefferson Community College*, 260 F.3d 671 (6ᵗʰ Cir. 2001)

In a case involving a professor who alleged he had been retaliated against (through dismissal) for exercising his free-speech rights, the Court noted that reasonable school officials should have known that such speech, when it is germane to the classroom subject matter and advances an academic message, is protected by the First Amendment. The professor used the words "nigger" and "bitch" during a classroom discussion to illustrate the impact of such words.

23. *Harris v. Forklift Systems, Inc.*, 510 U.S. 17 (1993)

In determining the standard under Title VII, the Court held that while it is not necessary to show tangible psychological injury, the conduct must be more than merely offensive and must be "severe or pervasive enough to create an objectively hostile or abusive work environment."

24. *Healy v. James*, 408 U.S. 169 (1972)

This is the foundational Supreme Court case regarding the recognition of student groups. During a period of extreme campus turmoil, Central Connecticut State University refused to recognize a chapter of Students for a Democratic Society, a group that had been involved in violent protests at other colleges and universities. The Supreme Court rejected the argument that recognition merely constituted the college's "stamp of approval" and held that denial of official recognition of a group, based on that group's viewpoints or upon speculation that the group *may* engage in punishable violence, violates the First Amendment's protection of freedom of association. The result of the denial of recognition was considered a form of "prior restraint" and once the group had met all the basic and legitimate (unrelated to viewpoint) requirements of recognition, the burden was on the school to justify its denial.

The Court noted that, "The College, acting here as the instrumentality of the State, may not restrict speech or association simply because it finds the views expressed by any group to be abhorrent."

The Court in this case quoted the *Tinker* case often and applied many of the protective principles of *Tinker* to the college environment. Quoting *Tinker,* "[u]ndifferentiated fear or apprehension of disturbance [which] is not enough to overcome the right to freedom of expression." *Tinker v. Des Moines Independent School District, 393 U.S., at 508.i*

The *Healy* Court does recognize the right of colleges and universities to deny recognition to groups that refuse to comply or to a student group that refuses to abide by reasonable rules governing behavior (as opposed to expression).

25. Hess v. Indiana, 414 U.S. 105 (1973)

In this case, the Court reversed the **disorderly conduct** conviction of a demonstrator who was arrested after the demonstration was broken up and said, "We'll take the fucking street later." The Court determined that the words must be intended and likely to produce imminent disorder in order to fall outside of the protection of the First Amendment. The demonstrator's words were not directed to any person and were not advocating any action and therefore were not imminent.

26. *Hustler Magazine v. Falwell*, 485 U.S. 46 (1988)

In *Hustler Magazine v. Falwell*, Jerry Falwell, a world-famous minister, brought a suit against *Hustler* magazine for intentional infliction of emotional distress for portraying him in a cartoon parody that suggested that he had an incestuous relationship with his mother and preached only when he was drunk. A jury awarded damages to Falwell for emotional distress, but the Supreme Court reversed the jury's decision and found that the parody was protected speech. The Court said that public figures (like Rev. Falwell) and public officials may not recover for intentional infliction of emotional distress without a showing of actual malice by the author of the parody because "such a standard is necessary to give adequate breathing space to the freedoms protected by the First Amendment."

27. *Iota Xi Chapter of Sigma Chi Fraternity v. George Mason University*, 993 F.2d 386 (1993)

In the *Iota Xi* case, a federal court acted to ensure that expression, even that deemed offensive or even "hostile" by some of those who witness the expression, remains protected by the First Amendment. In this case, Sigma Chi, a fraternity on the campus of George Mason University, held an "ugly woman" contest as part of an event that was intended to raise money for charity. As part of this contest, one of the fraternity members disguised himself as an overweight Black woman with pillows stuffed under his clothing and spoke in slang intended to parody African American speech patterns.

After student complaints, the university administration investigated the incident and ruled that the actions of the fraternity had "created a hostile learning environment" for women and Blacks and imposed serious sanctions on the fraternity. The fraternity then brought suit against the school to lift the sanctions. A federal appeals court ruled for Sigma Chi, determining that the fraternity member's appearance as an "ugly woman" was constitutionally protected expressive conduct despite its offensive nature and that the university's punishment of such conduct represented unconstitutional viewpoint discrimination.

28. *Keyishian v. Board of Regents*, 385 U.S. 589 (1967)

In *Keyishian*, the Court ruled that academic institutions cannot prohibit faculty, students, or staff from being members of organizations with which the institution's administration does not agree. In this case, a number of faculty and staff members of the State University of New York system brought a lawsuit against their employer for requiring that they reveal information on their political ideals under oath and on pain of dismissal. Faculty were required to reveal whether they had ever been a member of the Communist Party, while staff members were asked if they had ever been a member of an organization that preached the violent overthrow of the U.S. government (as the Communist Party did at that time).

In this case, the Supreme Court found that the oaths were vague and/or overbroad, and that both went against the spirit of freedom of academic inquiry. For instance, members of the Communist Party who did not believe in or try to bring about the violent overthrow of the government were being treated as though they did. Furthermore, the oaths effectively shut out of the university any person who did not subscribe to the official beliefs of the government, therefore severely curtailing academic freedom. Justice William J. Brennan wrote that "the vigilant protection of constitutional freedoms is nowhere more vital than in the community of American schools," and that academic freedom is "a special concern of the First Amendment, which does not tolerate laws that cast a pall of orthodoxy over the classroom."

29. *Lovelace v. Southeastern Massachusetts University*, 793 F.2d 419 (1ˢᵗ Cir. 1986)

The Court held that no constitutionally protected property or liberty interest was infringed when a professor's contract was not renewed without first affording him a hearing before his contract was not renewed. The Court noted that "by specifying in writing the usual criteria for promotion—teaching, scholarship, service—a university does not thereby set objective criteria, constricting its traditional discretion or transforming a largely judgmental decisional process into an automatic right to, or property interest in, tenure."

30. *Milkovich v. Lorain Journal Co.*, 497 U.S. 1 (1990)

In this case, the Court held that the First Amendment did not prohibit the application of Ohio's libel laws to the alleged defamation of a coach who sued when a newspaper printed an article implying that he had lied under oath. The Court said that there was no absolute privilege protecting opinion from the application of defamation laws. It said that the dispositive question was whether a reasonable fact finder could conclude that respondents' statements implied that petitioner had perjured himself.

31. *Miller v. California*, 413 U.S. 15 (1973)

In *Miller*, the Court laid out a three-part test for determining what materials were to be considered "obscene," and therefore not protected by the First Amendment. **The Court's test held that the basic guidelines to be considered were (a) whether "the average person,**

applying contemporary community standards" would find that
the work, taken as a whole, appeals to the prurient interest; (b)
whether the work depicts or describes, in a patently offensive
way, sexual conduct specifically defined by the applicable state
law; and (c) whether the work, taken as a whole, lacks serious literary, artistic, political, or scientific value. The Court held in *Miller*
that these standards were to be applied as guidelines to help the lower
courts determine what materials were obscene.

32. *New York Times v. Sullivan*, 376 U.S. 254 (1964)

In order to recover damages in a defamatory action, a public official must prove actual malice, which the Court says means the statement was made with the knowledge that it was false or with a reckless
disregard for whether it is true or not.

33. *New York Times v. United States*, 403 U.S. 713 (1971)

The Court ruled against the suppression of the Pentagon Papers,
despite the arguments that they would harm national security,
since the government did not meet the heavy burden necessary to
justify a prior restraint.

34. *Oncale v. Sundowner*, 523 U.S. 75 (1998)

The Court concluded that sex discrimination consisting of same-
sex sexual harassment is actionable under Title VII. In making this
determination, the Court noted, however, that the **"prohibition of
harassment on the basis of sex requires neither asexuality nor an-
drogyny in the workplace; it forbids only behavior so objectively
offensive as to alter the 'conditions' of the victim's employment."**

35. *Papish v. Board of Curators of the University of Missouri,* 410 U.S. 667 (1973)

In *Papish*, a student at the University of Missouri distributed a newspaper with a cartoon depicting policemen raping the Statue of Liberty and the Goddess of Justice. Inside the issue was an article entitled "Motherfucker Acquitted." The university expelled the student for violating a bylaw prohibiting "indecent conduct or speech." The Supreme Court overturned the student's expulsion, ruling that, "The mere dissemination of ideas—no matter how offensive to good taste— on a state university campus may not be shut off in the name alone of 'conventions of decency.'"

36. *Perry Education Association v. Perry Local Educators' Association,* 460 U.S. 37 (1983)

The Perry Education Association (PEA) was the elected exclusive bargaining unit for the teachers of the Metropolitan School District of Perry and a collective-bargaining agreement provided that PEA, but no other union, would have access to the inter-school mail system and teacher mailboxes in the Perry Township schools. The Court held that denying similar access to the mailbox did not violate free speech rights because mailboxes were not a public forum.

37. *Pickering v. Board of Education,* 391 U.S. 563 (1968)

In *Pickering*, the Court dealt with the protections of free speech for public employees. In that case, the Court held that a public school board violated the First Amendment when it fired a teacher for writing a letter to a local newspaper criticizing the expenditures made by the school. **Justice Thurgood Marshall held that the Court "unequivocally rejected [the notion] that teachers may constitutionally be** compelled to relinquish the First Amendment rights they would otherwise enjoy as citizens to comment on matters of public interest in connection with the operation of public schools in which they work." The Court did give credence, however, to the school's interest as an employer in "promoting the efficiency of the public services it performs through its employees" and held that the extent to which public employees would be protected by the principles of free speech depended on a balancing of the interests of the individual and the school.

38. *R.A.V. v. City of St. Paul*, 505 U.S. 377 (1992)

In *R.A.V.*, the city of St. Paul attempted to prosecute an individual under the city's "Bias-Motivated Crime Ordinance" for burning a cross in the yard of a Black family. The Court held in that case that the city's ordinance, which prohibited placing, on public or private property, "a symbol, object, appellation…which one knows or has reasonable grounds to know arouses anger, alarm or resentment in others on the basis of race, color, creed, religion or gender" was invalid **because it unconstitutionally prohibited "otherwise permitted speech solely on the basis of the subjects the speech addresses."** The Court overturned the conviction of the cross burner. The primary principle of this case is that even within an unprotected form of speech, the state may not choose to ban only those expressions whose viewpoints it dislikes. Readers of this case, of course, should not assume that there is no way to prevent cross-burning when that act is intended to convey a physical threat to person or property. *R.A.V.* is primarily concerned with the invalidity of the statute the prosecution was based on, not on the protected nature of the act.

39. *Robert J. Corry, et al. v. The Leland Stanford Junior University, et al.,* No. 740309 (California Super. Ct., Santa Clara County Feb. 27, 1995)

In *Corry*, a California state court struck down Stanford University's speech code because it banned speech that was protected by the Constitution. The university argued that the speech code prohibited only speech within the Supreme Court's doctrine of "fighting words" (see *Chaplinsky*, above), but the state court disagreed, holding that the speech forbidden by the university's code extended well beyond the bounds of "fighting words." Although Stanford argued that it was a private university and therefore could not be sued by the students for a violation of free-speech rights, the Court held that under California's "Leonard Law," which gives private university students the same Constitutional rights on campus as they would enjoy off campus, the policy violated the First Amendment rights of the students by its overbroad prohibitions on student speech.

40. *Rosenberger v. Rector and Visitors of the University of Virginia,* 515 U.S. 819 (1995)

In *Rosenberger*, the Court determined that religious groups on public campuses must be treated equally with non-religious groups. In this case, the University of Virginia had refused to fund a Christian newspaper started by some students on campus on the grounds that it would constitute an establishment of religion by the state. This determination was based solely on the fact that the paper was written from a Christian viewpoint rather than a secular one. Other student publications that did not claim to have a religious viewpoint were considered eligible for University funding.

The Supreme Court held that the university could not refuse to fund student religious activity while funding the publications of other organizations because such a regulation was based on the content of the message conveyed by the publication and was therefore impermissible viewpoint discrimination. The Supreme Court has consistently held that restricting speech on the basis of the viewpoint of the speaker will almost never pass constitutional muster. **For the majority, Justice Anthony Kennedy wrote that, "[h]aving offered to pay [the costs of printing] on behalf of private speakers who convey their own messages, the University may not silence the expression of selected viewpoints."**

41. Saxe v. State College Area School District, 240 F.3d 200 (3rd Cir. 2001)

In *Saxe*, a group of students challenged the constitutionality of a Pennsylvania public school district's "anti-harassment" policy as in violation of the First Amendment's guarantee of free speech. The students argued that the school district's policy against harassment violated their rights of free speech because they were Christians and that the school district's policy had the effect of silencing them because they feared that they would be punished for expressing their religious beliefs under the harassment policy. The Third Circuit Court held that the policy banning "harassing" speech used an unconstitutionally broad definition of what constituted "harassment" and remarked that there was "no categorical 'harassment exception' to the First Amendment's free speech clause."

42. Sons of Confederate Veterans, Inc. v. Commissioner of the Virginia DMV, 288 F.3d 610 (2002)

The Court held unconstitutional a provision in a Virginia statute that prohibited the Sons of Confederate Veterans from displaying any logo or emblem on the design of license plates that were issued under the statute whereas this restriction was not placed on other groups with special plates. The Court found that the logo restriction, which prevented the group from incorporating the Confederate flag into their plate design, was viewpoint discrimination.

43. *State v. Schmid*, 84 N. J. 535 (N. J., 1980)

In *Schmid*, defendant Chris Schmid was arrested on the campus of Princeton University for passing out political literature for the Labor Party in violation of a campus regulation that prohibited outsiders from soliciting on the Princeton campus. He was convicted of trespassing and appealed his conviction, contending that his arrest violated his state and federal rights of free speech. The Supreme Court of New Jersey overturned his conviction using a balancing test, saying that the campus of Princeton, despite being a private university, was sufficiently open to the public that the university could not totally eliminate Schmid's constitutional rights of free speech and assembly.

44. *Sweezy v. New Hampshire*, 354 U.S. 234 (1957)

In *Sweezy*, the Court suggested that teachers at the college and university level are protected by the First Amendment from having the content of their classroom speech regulated or examined by the legislature. Sweezy, a professor at the state university in New Hampshire, was subpoenaed and questioned about his activities with the Progressive Party and the content of his lectures. He refused to testify and was jailed, but the Supreme Court reversed his conviction and held that Sweezy was protected by the First Amendment from being compelled to testify and had a "right to lecture." The Court struck a bold blow for academic freedom in *Sweezy*, holding that "to impose any strait jacket upon the intellectual leaders in our colleges and universities would imperil the future of our nation...**Scholarship cannot flourish in an atmosphere of suspicion and distrust. Teachers and students must always remain free to inquire, to study and to evaluate.**"

45. *Terminiello v. Chicago*, 337 U.S. 1 (1949)

Father Arthur Terminiello, an orator, addressed a large crowd in a Chicago auditorium using inflammatory language. Outside the auditorium, over 1,000 people who were outraged by the speech given inside were protesting. Terminiello urged his audience inside the auditorium to defy the mob outside, calling those outside "communists," "snakes," and "scum." Terminiello was arrested and convicted for committing a breach of the peace. The Supreme Court reversed the conviction, holding that Terminiello's freedom of speech had been violated and arguing that "**[a] function of free speech under our system of government is to invite dispute.**" The Court further held that "**[s]peech is often provocative and challenging**" but is "**nevertheless protected against censorship or punishment.**"

46. *Texas v. Johnson*, 491 U.S. 397 (1989)

The Court upheld the right to burn the U.S. flag, noting that the government cannot reserve the flag for only those messages it wants to portray, in this case preserving it as a symbol of nationhood. "**If there is a bedrock principle underlying the First Amendment, it is that the government may not prohibit the expression of an idea simply because society finds the idea itself offensive or disagreeable.**"

47. *The UWM Post, Inc. v. Board of Regents of University of Wisconsin System*, 774 F. Supp. 1163 (D. Wis., 1991)

In *UWM Post*, several students challenged a speech code passed by the University of Wisconsin that forbade students from making comments that would "demean" others on the basis of a number of different categories such as race, gender, religion, etc. The university asserted that the policy was valid because it regulated only speech that could be considered "fighting words." **The Court disagreed, pointing out that "speech may demean an individual's characteristics without tending to incite that individual or others to an immediate breach of the peace," as required by *Chaplinsky*.** Since the code therefore forbade speech based solely on its content, the Court struck it down.

48. *Tinker v. Des Moines Independent School District*, 393 U.S. 503, 506 (1969)

Public high school officials suspended students because they wore black armbands to school in protest of the Vietnam War. The school and the lower court ruled that the ban was acceptable to prevent disruption of the school. **The Supreme Court ruled the high school's actions unconstitutional and stated that "in our system, undifferentiated fear or apprehension of disturbance is not enough to overcome the right to freedom of expression."** The Supreme Court recognized, however, that "conduct by the student, in class or out of it, which for any reason—whether it stems from time, place, or type of behavior—materially disrupts class work or involves substantial disorder or invasion of the rights of others is, of course, not immunized by the constitutional guarantee of freedom of speech." The mention of "time, place, and manner" means that speech, under certain circumstances, can be regulated by the state so long as the regulation is not

191

based on its viewpoint. "Viewpoint discrimination" is prohibited in virtually every circumstance involving state action.

Perhaps the most famous case regarding free speech in school, *Tinker*, which concerns a public high school, should be understood to create a floor to what administrators can do at public colleges but not understood to define the upper limits of collegiate free speech rights.

"It can hardly be argued that either students or teachers shed their constitutional rights to freedom of speech or expression at the schoolhouse gate." (*Tinker*, 1969)

The following is also interesting language for speech zone cases:

> "Freedom of expression would not truly exist if the right could be exercised only in an area that a benevolent government has provided as a safe haven for crackpots. The Constitution says that Congress (and the States) may not abridge the right to free speech. This provision means what it says. We properly read it to permit reasonable regulation of speech-connected activities in carefully restricted circumstances. But we do not confine the permissible exercise of First Amendment rights to a telephone booth or the four corners of a pamphlet, or to supervised and ordained discussion in a school classroom." (*Tinker,* 1969)

49. Virginia v. Black, 538 U.S. 343 (2003)

A plurality of the Court upheld a law that prohibited cross-burning with the intent to intimidate, noting that this is because some cross-burning constitutes a "true threat," which is constitutionally proscribable. The Court said that although some forms of cross-burning may be considered "intimidating" when carried out with the *intent* to communicate a threat of physical harm to a specific target, not all cross-burning may be automatically considered such a threat.

The Supreme Court has made it clear the kind of "intimidation" that states may lawfully forbid is "a type of true threat, where a speaker directs a threat to a person or group of persons with the intent of placing the victim in fear of bodily harm or death."

50. *Ward v. Rock against Racism*, 491 U.S. 781 (1989)

The Court determined that even in a public forum the government may place reasonable time, place, and manner restrictions but the government may not regulate expression in such a manner that a substantial portion of the burden on speech does not serve to advance its goals. However, while the restrictions should be narrowly tailored, it is not necessary that it be the least restrictive means of advancing the government's interest.

51. *West Virginia State Bd. of Ed. v. Barnette*, 319 U.S. 624 (1943)

In *Barnette*, the Supreme Court established so-called "negative" free speech rights. While free speech means having the ability to express one's own opinions without fear of punishment, *negative* free speech rights protect the right of the individual not to be compelled to express beliefs with which he or she disagrees. In *Barnette*, a group of elementary school students who were Jehovah's Witnesses refused to salute the flag as ordered by the state school board on the grounds that their religion prohibited this action. Their actions came in the middle of the darkest days of World War II, at a time when the very existence of our nation was threatened, and the board of education argued that a mandatory flag salute was necessary to foster national unity in that time of war.

Overturning a prior decision to the contrary, the Supreme Court stood up for the idea that even in times of crisis, the Constitutional rights of Americans must be respected. The Court forbade the school in question from expelling its students for refusing to salute the flag of the United States because they would have been forced to express a belief with which they did not agree. **Justice Jackson, who wrote the opinion of the Court, put it this way: "[i]f there is any fixed star in our constitutional constellation, it is that no official, high or petty, can prescribe what shall be orthodox in politics, nationalism, religion, or other matters of opinion or force citizens to confess by word or act their faith therein."**

52. *Widmar v. Vincent,* 454 U.S. 263 (1981)

The Court held that the university's exclusionary policy, which did not allow a registered student group to use a generally open forum to engage in religious worship and discussion, violated the fundamental principle that a state regulation of speech should be content-neutral.

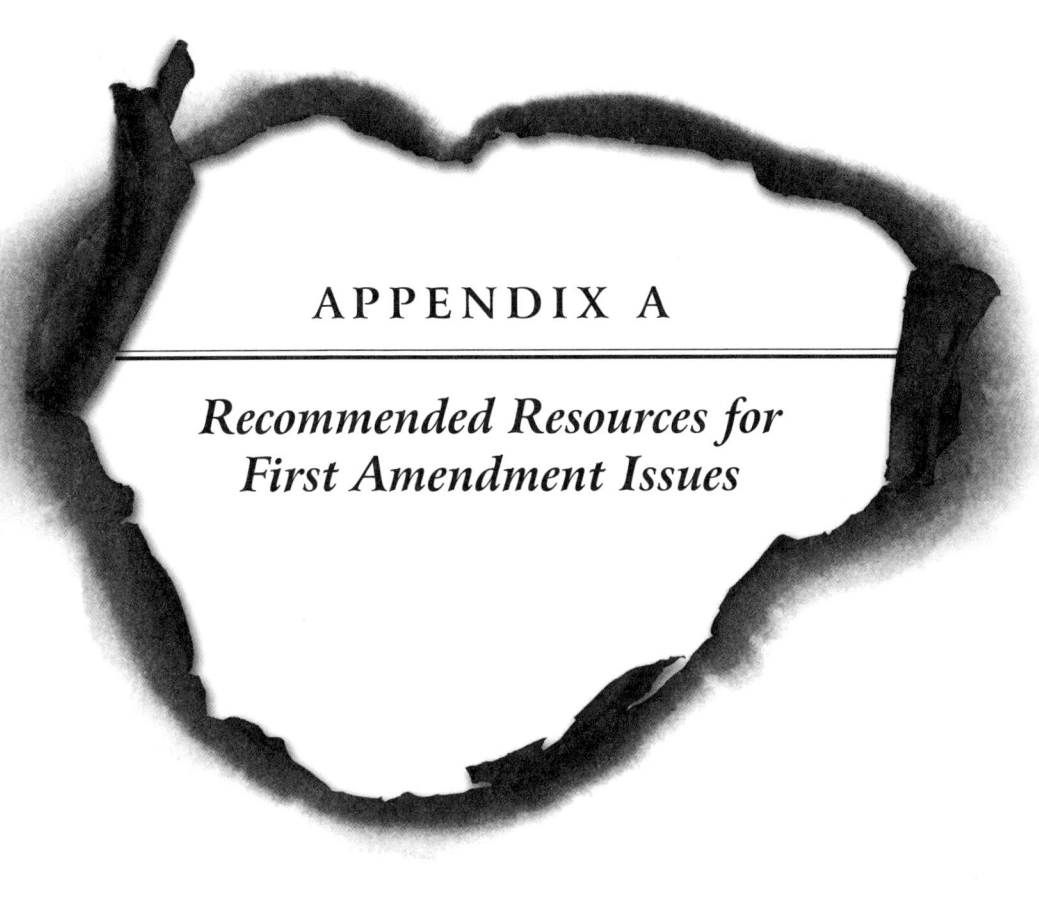

APPENDIX A

Recommended Resources for First Amendment Issues

APPENDIX A

OUTSIDE GROUPS FOCUSED ON CAMPUS FIRST AMENDMENT ISSUES

~~~~~~

Source: Alliance Defense Fund's Center for Academic Freedom (ADF)

Web site: http://www.alliancedefensefund.org

Address: 15333 North Pima Road Suite 165, Scottsdale, AZ 85260

Phone: (800) 835-5233

Mission: The Alliance Defense Fund is a legal alliance defending the right to aggressively defend religious liberty by empowering allies through strategy, funding, and litigation.

Services: The ADF is a servant organization that provides resources that strive to keep the door open for spreading the Gospel through the legal defense and advocacy of religious freedom, sanctity of human life, and traditional family values. The ADF is a legal ministry that provides training through an accredited academy program for practicing attorneys; funding for cases and legal projects; speakers; coordination an allied effort/resources; and litigation, support, and partnership for select cases.

~~~~~~

Source: Foundation for Individual Rights in Education (FIRE)

Web site: http://www.thefire.org

Address: 601 Walnut Street, Suite 510, Philadelphia, PA 19106

Phone: (215) 717-3473

Mission: The mission of FIRE is to defend and sustain individual rights at colleges and universities dealing with free speech, legal equality, due process, and religious liberty that have not been fairly protected. FIRE's core mission is to educate the public and community about the threats to these rights on college campuses.

Services: FIRE has published a *Guide to Free Speech on Campus*. Through personal subscription, FIRE sends periodic e-mail and fax updates regarding current cases, FIRE events, and issues of note as well as links to recent media coverage.

Source: Student Press Law Center (SPLC)

Web site: http://www.splc.org/

Address: 1101 Wilson Blvd, Suite 1100, Arlington, VA 22209

Phone: (703) 807-1904

Mission: The Student Press Law Center is an advocate for student free-press rights and provides information, advice, and legal assistance at no charge to students and the educators who work with them.

Services: SPLC members receive free legal advice and assistance on the legal issues affecting the student media. Members receive a subscription to the Student Press Law Center (SPLC) magazine, the *SPLC Report*, as well as the *SPLC Legal Alert*, and a members-only e-mail newsletter, which is published monthly from September through May. Members are entitled to a special price on copies of the book, *Law of the Student Press*, as well as access to the members-only online version. Members also receive free

SPLC packets, which they may reproduce for classroom use, and receive a discount on additional packets.

~~~~~~

Source: Students for Academic Freedom

Web site: http://www.studentsforacademicfreedom.org/

Address: 4401 Wilshire Blvd, 4th Floor, Los Angeles, CA 90010

Phone: (888) 527-3321

Mission: The Students for Academic Freedom Information Center is a clearinghouse and communications center for a national coalition of student organizations whose goal is to restore intellectual diversity on college campuses.

Services: Promotes student organizational chapters; provides a national office and coordinator in Washington D.C.; petitions legislators to enact an Academic Bill of Rights that will insist on intellectual diversity in the university curriculum; created a Web site to be a clearinghouse for this national coalition of students working to restore academic integrity and academic freedom to college campuses.

GENERAL FIRST AMENDMENT RESOURCES

~~~~~~

Source: First Amendment Center

Web site: http://www.firstamendmentcenter.org

Address: 1207 18th Ave. S., Nashville, TN 37212

E-mail: info@fac.org

Phone: (615) 727-1303

Mission: The First Amendment Center works to preserve and protect First Amendment freedoms through information and education. The center serves as a forum for the study and exploration of free expression issues, including freedom of speech, the press, and religion, and the rights to assemble and to petition the government. The center is an operating program of the Freedom Forum. Its affiliation with Vanderbilt University is through the Vanderbilt Institute for Public Policy Studies.

Services: The Center serves as a nonpartisan source of current information via the Web site (updated daily), speaking engagements, and participation in nonpartisan educational events. There is also a "First Amendment Center Online," which offers comprehensive research coverage of key First Amendment issues and topics, First Amendment news, a First Amendment Library, and guest analyses by respected legal specialists.

Source: Freedom Forum

Web site: http://www.freedomforum.org

Address: 1101 Wilson Blvd, Arlington, VA 22209

E-mail: news@freedomforum.org

Phone: (703) 528-0800

Mission: The Freedom Forum is a nonpartisan foundation dedicated to free press, free speech, and free spirit for all people. The foundation focuses on three priorities:

the Newseum, First Amendment freedoms, and newsroom diversity.

Services: The Freedom Forum funds the operations of the Newseum, an interactive museum of news under construction in Washington, D.C.; the First Amendment Center; and the Diversity Institute. The First Amendment Center and the Diversity Institute are housed in the John Seigenthaler Center at Vanderbilt University in Nashville, Tennessee. The First Amendment Center also has offices in Arlington, Virginia, and the Diversity Institute has offices and programs at the University of South Dakota in Vermillion.

Source: The Free Expression Policy Project (FEPP)

Web site: http://www.fepproject.org/index.html

Address: 161 Avenue of the Americas, 12th Floor, New York, NY 10013

Phone: (212) 998-6733

Mission: The Free Expression Policy Project, founded in 2000, provides research and advocacy on free speech, copyright, and media democracy issues. In May, 2004, FEPP became part of the Democracy Program at the Brennan Center for Justice at NYU School of Law.

Services: Primary areas of inquiry include restrictions on publicly funded expression; Internet filters, rating systems, and other measures that restrict access to information and ideas in the digital age; restrictive copyright laws, digital rights management, and other imbalances in the "intellectual property" system; mass media consolidation, public access to the airwaves, and other issues of media democracy; and censorship designed to "shield" adolescents and children from controversial art, information, and ideas.

~~~~~~

Source: Thomas Jefferson Center for the Protection of Free Expression

Web site: http://www.tjcenter.org/about.html

Address: 400 Worrell Drive, Charlottesville, VA 22911-8691

Phone: (434) 295-4784

Mission: The Thomas Jefferson Center for the Protection of Free Expression is a unique organization, devoted solely to the defense of free expression in all its forms.

Services: The Center serves as a source of information on speech and press issues; reaches out to the public through its conferences and colloquia; provides a First Amendment Case Conference Service; reunites key players in landmark free-speech cases to examine the impact of the decision; provides speakers for civic groups, bar associations, arts councils, schools, colleges, and universities and sponsors a First Amendment Clinic. (Note: There is an extensive list of links located within the "Contact Us" section.)

COURT RESOURCES

~~~~~~

Source: Supreme Court of the United States; The Oyez Project

APPENDIX A

Web site: http://www.oyez.org/oyez/frontpage

Services: The OYEZ Project is a multimedia archive devoted to the Supreme Court of the United States and its work. It aims to be a complete and authoritative source for all audio recorded in the Court since the installation of a recording system in October 1955. The project also provides authoritative information on all justices and offers a virtual reality tour of portions of the Supreme Court building, including the chambers of some of the justices.

~~~~~~

Source: THOMAS

Web site: http://thomas.loc.gov/

Services: THOMAS, a Web site of legislative information on the Internet, is a project of the Library of Congress and includes extensive legislative information, including search databases of pending legislation. The scope of this Web site includes bills, resolution, activity in Congress, Congressional Record, schedules and calendars, committee information, presidential nominations, treaties, and government resources.

RESOURCES FOR HIGHER EDUCATION

~~~~~~

Source: Association for Student Judicial Affairs (ASJA)

Web site: http://www.asjaonline.org/

Address: P.O. Box 2237, College Station, TX 77841-2237

Phone: (979) 845-5262

Mission: ASJA is an organization dedicated to the advancement of student conduct and student development in post-secondary educational settings. It is dedicated to promoting, encouraging, and educating student development professionals who have responsibility for student conduct.

Services: Membership in ASJA provides services that include a weekly *Law and Policy Report*, an annual international conference, Web site resources, circuit membership, committee involvement, consortium for government relations, the annual Gehring Student Judicial Affairs Training Institute, career listings, membership listserv/ discussion group, and research grants.

Source: Council on Law in Higher Education

Web site: http://www.clhe.org/

Address: 111 Coconut Key Court, Palm Beach Gardens, FL 33418

Phone: (561) 622-5765

Mission: The Council on Law in Higher Education (CLHE) is an independent nonprofit organization, founded in 1998, that is dedicated to assisting presidents, senior-level administrators, and attorneys in managing legal risk and improving regulatory compliance.

Services: CLHE provides a variety of publications and programs, offers assistance to higher education institutions in meeting legal and regulatory requirements, advocates for public policy solutions and legal reforms and promotes student rights.

203

Source:	NASPA–Student Affairs Administrators in Higher Education
Web site:	http://www.naspa.org/
Address:	1875 Connecticut Avenue, NW, Suite 418, Washington, DC 20009-5728
Phone:	(202) 265-7500
Mission:	NASPA is the leading voice for student affairs administration, policy, and practice and affirms the commitment of student affairs to educating the whole student and integrating student life and learning.
Services:	Professional development to members through high-quality experiences, information, and exemplary models of practice; leadership in higher education through policy development and advocacy for students on important international, national, state, and local issues; advancement of pluralism, diversity, and internationalism in NASPA and the profession; leadership for promoting, assessing, and supporting student learning and successful educational outcomes; and maintenance, evaluation, and development of a high-quality association structure and national office to meet current needs, anticipate future trends, and promote growth.

Source:	LRP Publications
Web site:	http://www.lrp.com/
Address:	360 Hiatt Drive, Palm Beach Gardens, FL 33418
Phone:	(800) 341-7874

Services: LRP Publications offers *Student Affairs Today*, a short, user-friendly newsletter on current issues and cases. Reprint requests, multiple-copy discounts and back orders.

APPENDIX B

ASJA
First Amendment Survey

A national survey on free expression issues on college campuses was conducted in spring 2005. The survey, targeted for current members of the Association for Student Judicial Affairs (ASJA) listserv, resulted in 381 responses. The goal of the survey was to determine knowledge and comfort levels surrounding First Amendment issues at colleges and universities. The following is a brief synopsis of the survey's primary findings.

Of the 381 responses, 65% of the respondents represented public colleges or universities; 23% represented private schools while 11% represented private religious institutions. Of those completing the survey, 1% did not respond to this question. The following chart reveals actual numbers representing the public, private, and private religious institutions.

Type of Institutions

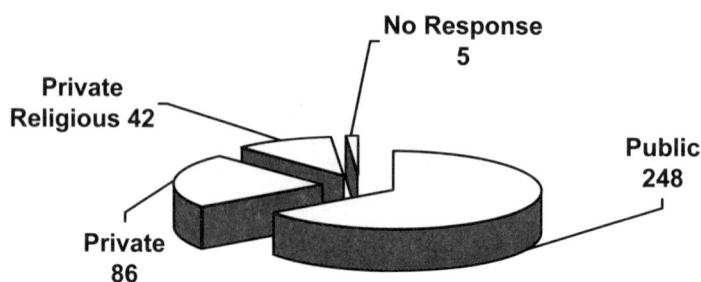

No Response
5

Private
Religious 42

Public
248

Private
86

The largest number of those completing the survey represented institutions with enrollments of 5,000 or below with 112 responses or 29.5%, followed by campuses over 20,000 with 89 respondents (23%). Institutions with 5,001 to 10,000 were next with 77 responses (20%).

Sixty-three respondents (16.5%) came from institutions with enrollments of 10,001–15,000. The smallest number of respondents, 40 or
11%, represented institutions with enrollments of 15,001–20,000.

Institutional Enrollments

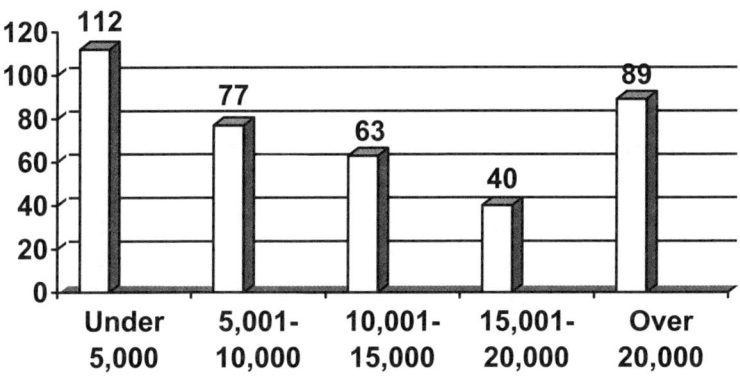

Survey results reflected an equal representation from all judicial
circuits. The following chart highlights the number of respondents
from those regions. While First Amendment applications do not apply
outside the United States, one respondent represented Canada. States
representing the judicial circuits are as follows:

Circuit 1:

Maine, Massachusetts, New Hampshire, Rhode Island

Circuit 2:

Connecticut, New York, Vermont

Circuit 3:

Delaware, New Jersey, Pennsylvania

Circuit 4:

South Carolina, North Carolina, Virginia, West Virginia, Maryland, Washington D.C.

Circuit 5:

Mississippi, Louisiana, Texas

Circuit 6:

Tennessee, Kentucky, Ohio, Michigan

Circuit 7:

Illinois, Indiana, Wisconsin

Circuit 8:

Arkansas, Missouri, Iowa, Nebraska, Minnesota, South Dakota, North Dakota

Circuit 9:

Arizona, California, Nevada, Oregon, Washington, Idaho, Montana, Alaska, Hawaii

Circuit 10:

Oklahoma, Kansas, New Mexico, Colorado, Utah, Wyoming

Circuit 11:

Florida, Alabama, Georgia

Judicial Circuits Represented

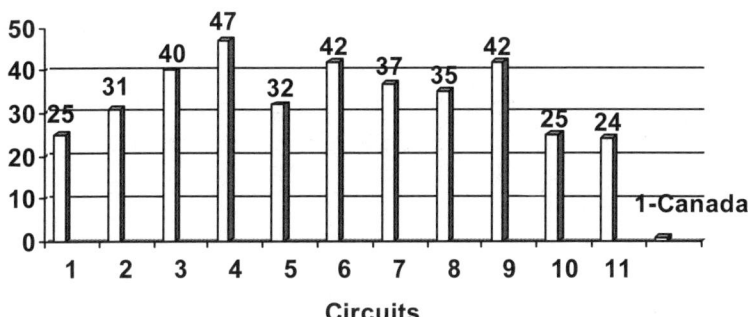

The survey reflects an array of administrative roles as suggested by the 381 responses. Most responses represent judicial officers (108 or 29%), deans or assistant deans (102 or 27%), and residence life personnel (81 or 21%). The following charts identify primary administrative roles and years of service to the profession as reported in the survey.

Primary Administrative Role

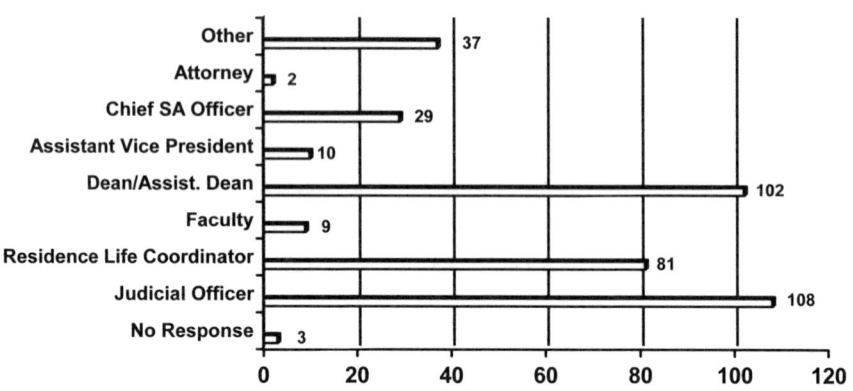

of Respondents/Years in Profession

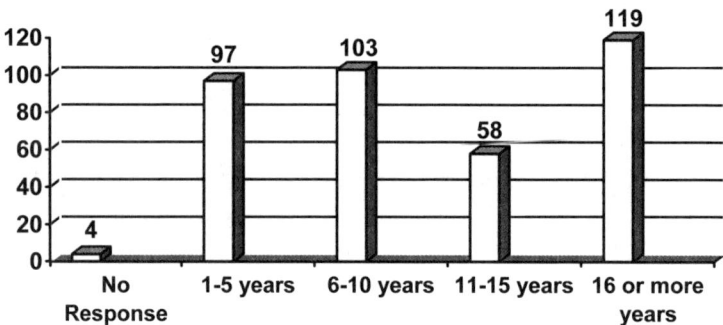

SURVEY QUESTIONS

1. Has your current campus ever faced First Amendment/free speech legal challenges involving any of the areas listed below?

Check all that apply:

- ★ Legal Challenges

- ★ Hate Speech

- ★ Campus Speaker

- ★ Speech Zones

- ★ Preacher

- ★ Group Recognition

- ★ Group Fee

- ★ Campus Newspaper

- ★ Sexual Harassment

- ★ Racial Harassment

- ★ Campus Protests

- ★ Academic Freedoms

- ★ Other

Overall, most respondents (227 or 60%) indicated that no "legal challenges" had surfaced regarding the First Amendment topics identified above while 134 (35%) indicated that some challenges had been addressed. Twenty individuals, (5%), did not respond to the initial question. When asked about each topic separately, the responses were as follows:

Hate Speech

Yes	31
No	343
No Response	7

Group Recognition

Yes	32
No	342
No Response	7

Racial Harassment

Yes	30
No	344
No Response	7

Campus Speaker

Yes	40
No	334
No Response	7

Group Fee

Yes	11
No	363
No Response	7

Campus Protest

Yes	21
No	353
No Response	7

Speech Zones

Yes	53
No	321
No Response	7

Campus Newspaper

Yes	33
No	341
No Response	7

Academic Freedom

Yes	14
No	360
No Response	7

Preacher

Yes	27
No	347
No Response	7

Sexual Harassment

Yes	37
No	337
No Response	7

Other*

Yes	15
No	359
No Response	7

*Including campus e-mail, campaign speech, GLBT/religious, radio station, yearbook content, campus movies

2. Has your current campus ever faced First Amendment/free speech policy grievances/complaints involving any of the areas listed below? Check all that apply:

This question inquired if "policy grievances/complaints" had been reported regarding the same topics as listed in Question 1. When responding to this question, an overwhelming majority of the responses

(264 or 69%) stated that "grievances/complaints" had been reported while 87 (23%) reported no. Thirty (8%) did not respond to the initial question. The following results were reported when asked about each specific topic:

Hate Speech

Yes	128
No	249
No Response	4

Group Recognition

Yes	81
No	296
No Response	4

Racial Harassment

Yes	107
No	270
No Response	4

Campus Speaker

Yes	116
No	261
No Response	4

Group Fee

Yes	36
No	341
No Response	4

Campus Protest

Yes	67
No	310
No Response	4

Speech Zones

Yes	70
No	308
No Response	3

Campus Newspaper

Yes	111
No	266
No Response	4

Academic Freedom

Yes	55
No	222
No Response	4

Preacher

Yes	71
No	306
No Response	4

Sexual Harassment

Yes	123
No	254
No Response	4

Other*

Yes	17
No	360
No Response	4

*Including radio station, fans/athletic event, classroom art, campus elections, Web site content, displays, movie content, graphic posters, use of facilities, hiring practices, profanity on posters, fraternity photos, low grades because of religious views

3. Please rate your general familiarity with First Amendment case law affecting higher education:

Minimal ... Somewhat ... Adequate ... Good ... Excellent

The following chart reflects how respondents felt about "familiarity" with First Amendment case law. Cumulative percentages indicate that only 36.5% were in the "minimal to somewhat" range while 55.9%

felt their familiarity was "adequate to excellent." Specific results of the 381 responding to the survey are as follows:

Familiarity with First Amendment Law

	#	Percent	Cumulative Percent
Minimal	45	11.8%	11.8%
Somewhat	94	24.7%	36.5%
Adequate	99	26.0%	62.5%
Good	87	22.8%	85.3%
Excellent	27	7.1%	92.4%
No Response	29	7.6%	100.0%

When asked about familiarity with specific topics, responses varied. The following indicates weaknesses and strengths in the "minimal to somewhat" and "adequate to excellent" range. "No Response" entries for these topics ranged from 4 (1.0%) to 11 (2.9%). Total responses equal 381. Percentages in **bold** indicate where responses of 50 percent or higher prevailed.

Topic	#	Minimal to Somewhat	#	Adequate to Excellent
Public Forum	175	(45.9%)	202	**(53.1%)**
Chilling Effect	228	**(59.8%)**	143	(37.6%)
Legal Limits	144	(37.8%)	228	**(59.9%)**
Breadth/Vagueness	210	**(55.1%)**	163	(42.8%)
Time/Place/Manner	113	(29.4%)	262	**(68.8%)**
Harassment v. Hurtful Speech	121	(31.7%)	253	**(66.4%)**
Content Neutrality	185	(48.5%)	190	(49.9%)
Freedom of Press	112	(29.3%)	259	**(68.0%)**

Prior Restraint	235	**(61.7%)**	136	(37.5%)
Defamation	176	(46.2%)	196	**(51.5%)**
Captive Audience	221	**(58.0%)**	149	(39.1%)
Viewpoint Discrimination	231	**(60.6%)**	142	(37.3%)

4. Please rate your comfort level in discussing First Amendment issues with the constituents listed below using the following scale:

Very Uncomfortable ... Uneasy ... OK ... Comfortable ... Very Comfortable

Constituent groups listed in the survey as a response to this question included the following groups. Responses in the "OK to Very Comfortable" range are listed adjacent to each constituent group. Comfort levels with students and student leaders ranked the highest followed closely by administrators, faculty, and the general public. The lowest comfort levels were with board of trustees/regents and media/ newspapers.

★   Individual Students (89.2%)

★   Student Leaders (84.2%)

★   Faculty (73.8%)

★   Administrators (79.8%)

★   Board of Trustees/Regents (58.8%)

★   General Public (72.4%)

★   Media/Newspaper (62.0%)

ASJA members were asked:

When you have questions about free speech/First Amendment issues, where do you turn for information?

Of the 381 individuals that responded to the survey, a large percentage (60.9% or 232) stated they would seek out other ASJA colleagues for information while 29.1% (111 respondents) stated they would turn to publications. Publications listed by those completing the survey included:

American Civil Liberties Union (ACLU) publications

Association for Student Judicial Affairs (ASJA) *Law and Policy Report* and Web site

The Chronicle of Higher Education

College Student/Administrator and the Courts

Council on Law in Higher Education (CLHE)

Ed.gov Web site

Foundation for Individual Rights in Education (FIRE) books and Web site

Fraternity Law

Higher Education Law in America

Higher Education Legal Alert

Kaplin and Lee's *The Law in Higher Education*

Kent Week's *Student Handbook Policies*

Journal of College and University Law

Law and Policy Report

Legal Issues for the Student Affairs Professional

Lexis-Nexis

Law & Policy Review

National Association of Student Personnel Administrators (NAS-PA) journals

National On-Campus Report

Student Services and the Law

Oakstone's *Higher Education Law*

On-Campus Report

Perspective

Student Affairs Today

Student Organizational and Community Issues

Synfax

Synthesis

When asked separately, other sources that ranked high as contacts included campus attorney (307 or 80.6%), supervisors (213 or 55.9%), and legal research (160 or 42%). "Other" sources identified included administrators, residence life staff, law school faculty, public safety directors, First Amendment Centers, national fraternity offices, and an array of personal contacts and professional colleagues.

Private school members were asked:

State action is a doctrine of constitutional law which imposes constitutional obligations upon private entities that somehow

act in place of the state. How familiar are you with the state action doctrine?

Minimal ... Somewhat ... Adequate ... Good ... Excellent

Of the 160 respondents representing the 86 private and 42 private religious institutions completing the survey, 89 (23.4%) expressed "minimal" familiarity with the state action doctrine. Twenty-nine (7.6%) expressed "somewhat" familiarity, 20 (5.2%) expressed "adequate" familiarity, 12 (3.1%) expressed "good" familiarity, and 10 (2.6%) expressed "excellent" familiarity.

When separating private and private-religious responses from the survey, data mirrored findings found in the overall results when comparing "legal challenges" to "grievances/complaints." The following is a brief example of how these institutions reported data.

Has your current campus ever faced First Amendment/free speech legal challenges involving any of the areas listed below? Check all that apply:

Topic	Private (86 responses)	Private Religious (42 responses)
Some Legal Challenges	17 or 19.8%	7 or 16.7%
Hate Speech	6 or 7.0%	2 or 4.8%
Campus Speaker	9 or 10.5%	2 or 4.8%
Speech Zones	2 or 2.3%	0 or 0.0 %
Preacher	2 or 2.3%	1 or 2.4%
Group Recognition	7 or 8.1%	1 or 2.4%
Group Fee	2 or 2.3%	1 or 2.4%
Campus Newspaper	5 or 5.8%	2 or 4.8%
Sexual Harassment	4 or 4.7%	3 or 7.1%
Racial Harassment	4 or 4.7%	1 or 2.4%

Campus Protest	4 or 4.7%	0 or 0.0%
Academic Freedom	1 or 1.2%	0 or 0.0%
Other	2 or 2.3%	1 or 2.4%

Similar to the overall findings, private and private religious institutions reported a sharp increase when reporting on "policy grievances/complaints." Specifically, the question asked:

Has your current campus ever faced First Amendment/free speech policy grievances/complaints involving any of the areas listed below? Check all that apply:

Topic	Private (86 responses)	Private Religious (42 responses)
Grievances/Complaints	54 or 62.8%	29 or 69.0%
Hate Speech	20 or 23.3%	11 or 26.2%
Campus Speaker	22 or 25.6%	8 or 19.0%
Speech Zones	15 or 17.4%	9 or 21.4%
Preacher	5 or 5.8%	3 or 7.1%
Group Recognition	13 or 15.1%	9 or 21.4%
Group Fee	4 or 4.7%	1 or 2.4%
Campus Newspaper	17 or 19.8%	11 or 26.2%
Sexual Harassment	23 or 26.7%	12 or 28.6%
Racial Harassment	15 or 17.4%	13 or 31.0%
Campus Protest	9 or 10.5%	5 or 11.9%
Academic Freedom	6 or 7.0%	3 or 7.1%
Other	6 or 7.0%	2 or 4.8%

Note: Similar data was collected and analyzed by institutional enrollment categories and by judicial circuits.

CONTRIBUTORS

Lee E. Bird, PhD, is the vice president for student affairs at Oklahoma State University. She served as president for the Association for Student Judicial Affairs in 2003–04 and serves regularly as an instructor at the Donald D. Gehring Judicial Affairs Institute.

Mary Beth Mackin, MSEd, is the assistant dean of student life at the University of Wisconsin–Whitewater. She is a long-time member of the Association for Student Judicial Affairs, having served as president in 2006–07 and as treasurer from 2002–04.

Saundra K. Schuster, Esq., is an assistant attorney general for the state of Ohio and serves as the general counsel for Sinclair Community College. She is a charter member of the Association for Student Judicial Affairs and served as president of the association in 1997. She is a graduate of the Michael E. Moritz College of Law at The Ohio State University.

Elizabeth M. Baldizan, EdD, is the director of the Jean Nidetch Women's Center at the University of Nevada–Las Vegas. She served as president of the Association for Student Judicial Affairs from 1999–2000 and as a faculty member at the association's Donald D. Gehring Training Institute in 2005. She has served on the board of directors for the National Association of Student Personnel Administrators and on the editorial board for the Council on Law in Higher Education's *Student Affairs Law and Policy* publication.

Roger R. Lee, PhD, is vice president for student affairs and dean of students at Reinhardt College in Waleska, Georgia. He has served in a number of student service positions at colleges and universities throughout the southeast. His *Freedom of Expression: A Model Policy on Free Speech, Campus Protests, Demonstrations, and Speakers for the Public*

University Community received the Dissertation of the Year Award from the Association for Student Judicial Affairs in 2004.

Greg C. Lukianoff, Esq., is an attorney and the president of the Foundation for Individual Rights in Education (FIRE). He has published articles on campus free speech in *The Boston Globe*, the *New York Post*, *The Chronicle of Higher Education*, *Fraternal Law*, *Inside Higher Ed*, and numerous other publications. Greg is a graduate of American University and of Stanford Law School, where he focused on First Amendment and constitutional law.